THE MAGIC OF Tea

Ms Karryn Gina Bond.

Christmas 2022 from V.

(With a tea i Biscuit. cup, mug, Tray
(with Legs) For 1)

THE MAGIC
OF
Tea

ALICE PARSONS

FOREWORD BY
NICHOLAS SHAKESPEARE

JCP

First published by
Jane Curry Publishing 2012
[Wentworth Concepts Pty Ltd]
PO Box 780 Edgecliff NSW 2027 Australia

www.janecurrypublishing.com.au

National Library of Australia Cataloguing-in-Publication entry

Author:	Parson, Alice.
Title:	The Magic of Tea/Alice Parsons;
	introduction by Nicholas Shakespeare.
ISBN:	9780987227560 (hbk.)
Subjects:	Tea.
	Tea--History.
	Cooking (Tea)
	Tea tasting.
Dewey Number:	641.3372

Design: Cheryl Collins Design
Printed in China by Jade Productions

Dedication

This book is dedicated
with love to my precious
family and friends who
have all helped me
unstintingly as
The Magic of Tea
has been realised, like the
best of tea, from its first
flush to full bloom.

Contents

Foreword by
Nicholas Shakespeare

We all of us have our goat-paths. My own takes me once a week on Saturday morning through the centre of Oxford to the Cardew's stall in the corner of the covered market. Out of large tin tea-caddies, inlaid with Chinese scenes, my week ahead is measured and then poured into small white packets on which Nikki behind the counter scribbles Oxford Breakfast or Darjeeling or Ceylon or Chai or Nepal, according to my mood. Any deviation is fraught with peril. It made for a black letter day when I was told that Cardew's had run out of Antu Valley Tea ('Maoist guerrillas'), and expected no further consignments. I felt I had lost a taste bud.

Of all the terrific things that one can say about tea, it is the ritual that it demands of its lovers which I find seductive. About fifteen years ago, I was invited on a writers' tour to Vienna, by a long stretch the junior member of a group of novelists each with their own strong and distinctive flavour. I recall a member of the audience asking Julian Barnes the question of questions: 'Why do you write?' And his very good answer: 'Because it's the most serious thing I can do.' I repressed a diabolic urge to stick up my hand to ask the question that I have come to regard as even more revelatory of the creative process: 'How do you take your tea?'

Once in a novel I introduced a magic Berber teapot, the property of a dancing girl from the Ait Haddidu. One night in the Rif she danced around a fire before three students. She held the teapot to the face of the first.

'What do you drink?' Her eyes mocked him. They had been emboldened with antimony and her eyebrows arched with soot. There were indigo tattoos on her chin.

Champagne, he joked. He held up his metal mug. The girl lowered the camel-neck spout and poured.

It wasn't vintage, and it was warm. But it was champagne.

The student next to him asked for vodka.

And what came out? Vodka! The action was repeated, this time with wine, after which the third student determined to buy this miraculous vessel. The girl refused. It was an heirloom. She stroked the lid, mocking him. It had passed from her family when her ancestors defeated King Sebastian. It had belonged to the ten-year-old Duke of Barcelos. It had been made in Cordoba under Abd-ar-Rachman III. 'It is magic.'

He held out the mug for more. Again she poured. She could name her price, he said. She shook her head, jingling

with armillae. He mentioned a price that she could name. The bracelets jingled again. He raised his offer. The fire was dying out when her head grew still and she parted with her magic heirloom. He took the teapot to bed.

The girl was gone when he woke, so he was unable to question her about the words engraved on its base which included the name of an industrial town in northern England.

Why did I choose a teapot? Because nothing is more familiar and inoffensive — is anything less threatening than a tea-cosy? And yet, in the same gulp, nothing is more capable of transporting you from your humdrum surroundings to the earth's wonderful places, and binding you to them. Tea is truly international. The word for it is virtually the same in every language. It is the Esperanto of tastes. You can brew it out of anything — from mint leaves to ginger. Its vocabulary has percolated into our everyday expressions. You can even brew a cold. But the beneficial effect of drinking tea is by and large the same. 'Anywhere a person cultivates tea, long life will follow,' believed the thirteenth-century Buddhist monk, Eisai. 'In ancient and modern times, tea is the elixir that makes the mountain-dwelling immortal.'

To paraphrase a coffee-drinker, Dr Johnson, someone who is sick of tea is sick of life. They are sad and unrescuable. They will miss out on everything associated with tea. They will miss out on marmalade, boiled eggs, scones, mint julep, toad-in-the-hole, green-tea ice-cream, cucumber sandwiches, Welsh rarebit — even coffee. They will miss out on the conversations that you have over 'a cuppa'; on the relationships that form, the enemies that can be pacified. They will miss out on the places that tea, like a camera, enables you to retain long after you have put down your cup.

For some mysterious reason, I still remember the places where I have drunk tea. I have taken it in a tent on the Tibetan border — 'bed-tea' out of an aluminium flask; through a perforated silver straw on the pampas — *yerba maté*, milkless, drawn up out of a dried gourd; in West Mavern out of willow-pattern porcelain bought back by my grandmother from Peking where she lived in the 1930s — she liked her tea strong enough, she said, to stand her spoon in it; out of a billy-can on Maria Island in Tasmania, where the south-easterly is so fierce that it can, as the locals say, blow the milk right out of your tea. I knew that I was at home in Hobart when I discovered in Liverpool Street the Antipodean equivalent of Cardew's: Jeffersons Tea.

I do not regret that I never asked Julian Barnes the real question of questions. Or indeed any of the questions on the tip of my tongue. (Do you take it with lemon — a habit introduced to the English by Queen Victoria, who pinched it off her Russian cousins? With milk? Do you put the milk in first, or after? Do you take sugar?

Brew it in a metal pot or porcelain?
Or in a single-cup mesh, as I have
taken to doing — you waste less tea?
Do you ever drink it iced? Read your
fortune in its leaves?). I am glad that
I managed to show the reticence and
patience which is another characteristic
of the tea-drinker, because Alice
Parsons answers not only all my
questions but many others that I could
never have imagined posing. Her book
is the tea-bible which I have been
seeking without realising that I was all
the while looking for it, like all the
best things.

The Magic of Tea

Magic is often stirred by memory. Or is it that memory is often stirred by magic? When I was musing about tea not long ago my father lifted his head and gently and proudly recited from memory the following lines:

'When the tea is brought in at five o'clock,
And all the neat curtains are drawn with care,
The little black cat with the bright green eyes
Is suddenly purring there.'

Extract from 'Milk For The Cat' by Harold Munro 1879–1932

Introduced to me in this way by my father, the little black cat with the bright green eyes has become my magical tea muse.

Introduction

The magic of tea for me lies in its extraordinary versatility and its generosity. It lifts us up when we need a boost, it fortifies and sometimes heals us; it unites us with those we love, and its healthy properties assist us in myriad unexpected ways. It can be exotic, sometimes mysterious and often intoxicatingly fragrant. And yet tea is also earthy, basic and uncomplicated. It can be enjoyed as much in an enamel mug by a campfire or building site as it can in exquisite fine bone china in a Japanese teahouse.

For nearly a year I have been gently exploring in and around the subject of this exceptional leaf and all that it engenders, and I am astonished by the range of its powers. I am still uncovering pearls of wisdom. I am still being startled and inspired, and that in itself is a joy. This book is a bit like *Camellia sinensis* herself, the tea tree, the starting point from where this story unfurls. For there are branch-like twists and turns as I take a look not only at tea but its related history, mythology, usage and customs. Also, I draw on a range of recipes that connect me with family and friends here and abroad, and in some manner with the mistress of this story, tea. Take your time, and a cuppa, while you peek into the labyrinth that is tea.

Alice Parsons
November 2012

Alice lives with her husband Anthony in rural New South Wales.

Chapter 1

Tea for two

At the beginning of the day a good cup of tea is essential or better still, a pot of tea. Sally, a good friend of mine, says that tea is the glue in her marriage. I could only agree. The time-honoured ritual of a husband offering his wife a cup of tea in bed each morning literally throws open the door on a day full of promise. My morning starts best with a cup of *Lapsang Souchong*. This is a strong and gutsy Chinese black tea. I put milk with it and have it piping hot.

Lapsang Souchong originally came from the *WuYi* mountains of China's Fujian province. The tea leaves are dried in the smoke from pine or cypress wood fires and it is this practice that gives them their distinctive (in my case addictive) smoky flavour. Records of *Lapsang Souchong* date back to the *Qing* Dynasty (1644–1911). Apparently, seeking shelter, a troop of soldiers commandeered a tea factory and so interrupted the normal production routine of the tea workers. These workers were then under pressure to get their tea dried in time to sell it at market. To expedite the process they force dried the leaves over pine wood fires. The resulting smoky tea was an instant local hit and very soon an international one too.

It is rumoured that it was *Lapsang Souchong* that was barrelled into Boston Harbour in the cavalcade of events surrounding the Boston Tea Party in 1773. (342 chests of it.)

A debt of gratitude

Tea was introduced to the court in Britain in 1662 when Charles II married the Portuguese Catherine of Braganza. (Holland and Portugal had already been importing it for half a century.) It was perceived as rare and precious. However awareness of it slowly spread, and it was taken up outside of the court by apothecaries, coffee houses and snuff shops. It remained exorbitantly expensive.

Teapots

The first teapots as we know them with their tiny matching cups, accompanied the tea brought to Europe by Chinese merchants in the seventeenth century. So-called *Yixing* pottery caused a thrill, as it was so much more refined than any European equivalent. It was translucent with a delicate purple colour: something of a contrast to the more coarse earthenware of the day.

Teapots today are another story. The range is boundless. It is in fact spectacular. Designers have produced ingenious vessels all in the name of the pot. And we the consumers can take our pick. My own favourite is a rooster pot purchased at a country fair. It steeps tea perfectly, is extremely decorative and does everything short of crow. And when it's not in the business of steeping, it is providing a very comfortable home for cut flowers.

Fat old brown Betty, I have learnt, is a pet name given to commonplace teapots. We have had one in the cupboard for years and I never realised she had a name. Betty is much loved and much used and does not dare compete with the rooster, but knows she has no need to.

Of course once you plan on brewing tea, you need a safe house for your leaves. Enter the tea caddy and other tea-phernalia.

Tea-phernalia of the seventeenth and eighteenth centuries

Once tea was on the scene in Europe, it was *de rigueur* for those who could meet the expense (as in the early years it really was an extremely costly commodity) to also possess all the elaborate accessories, what I call the *tea-phernalia* to go with it. And this fervour even carried as far as tea gowns, for there were not only tea parties but also tea dances. Tea was fashionable. It was exotic and romantic. It was a status symbol. It was in demand. And thankfully it has provided for us today an amazing legacy of artefacts, as craftsmen and artists of the time lent their talent to creating a stunning array of tea-associated treasures.

Tea caddies

The tea caddy began life as a canister fashioned in brass, silver or porcelain and evolved into finely crafted wooden boxes which would house compartments for storing tea canisters and then a vessel (usually made of glass) in which to make up your preferred blend.

Mote spoons and caddy spoons

Mote spoons (the forebears of caddy spoons) were designed and used to clear tea leaves of its dust, or mote. (Tea in the seventeenth century was quite crude and dusty.) They were fine long-handled spoons with delicately pierced bowls to allow dust to be sifted out from the leaves before their being brewed. And there is more; the long pointed handles on mote spoons were ideally suited to pushing tea leaves down the spout where as we all know they sometimes choose to lodge themselves.

Caddy spoons derived their shape from the scallop shell. Some early ones like the mote spoon also had fine filigree while dust was still an issue. Caddy spoons were made in treen, tortoiseshell, pearl, ivory, bone, brass, silver plate and sterling silver.

There are such treasures surrounding the rituals of tea drinking. And a vision still sits in my mind … of little girls sitting with tea sets and while they are not drinking tea, and nor are their dolls, they are swept away by the magic of it all.

A consumable treasure, Katrina's marmalade

A pantry, or indeed breakfast table (or tray) is incomplete without a pot of marmalade. Until a few years ago I had never attempted to make my own but my friend Katrina's simple recipe was all I needed to set the record straight. Making my own delighted me and I can only encourage others to try it too. It is not hard (as I had presumed) and the rewards are just that, rewarding. And naturally, homemade marmalade improves the taste of your tea immeasurably.
Makes 8 to 10 jars depending on size

Ingredients:

1kg finely sliced citrus with excess pith cut out and pips saved for soaking as described below (Six oranges and one large

17

grapefruit are Katrina's recommendation, but you can make up your own blend of fruits)
15 cups water
¼ cup squeezed lemon juice
1.8kg sugar

Method:

Soak finely-sliced fruit in water overnight. Soak pips in lemon juice overnight, too.

Bring water with soaked fruit up to the boil in a large heavy-bottomed saucepan. Remove from heat and add sugar, stirring until dissolved.

Add lemon juice and pips (placed in either a muslin bag or a pop sock). You can attach your pip-pouch, whether muslin or pop sock, to the side of your cooking pot with a piece of string. This makes for easier retrieval later.

Return to the heat and boil for half an hour give or take. Lower heat and keep bubbling for another half hour or so until the marmalade reaches setting point.

It is impossible to be precise about the timing here, but to check the marmalade has reached setting point you need simply to put a teaspoon of it onto a cool saucer and into the fridge for five minutes. Then you nudge the surface of the marmalade. If it wrinkles it is ready and you can wind up the cooking process. If the marmalade runs in the saucer, you need to continue boiling it until that skin forms. This can mean upwards of an hour or even more.

(I think altitude or attitude may have something to do with it as every time I cook marmalade, the time required for it to set varies so please never panic if time is marching and setting point is elusive. Do not be tempted to decant the marmalade before it is ready otherwise you will find yourself having to pour it all back and start all over again.)

Once the cooking process is complete, allow your marmalade to cool for a while and then decant it into a sterilised wide-rimmed jug and pour the contents from there into sterilised jars. The volume of marmalade produced here also varies, but in general it would fill about eight to ten average jars.

TIP At Christmas I prepare this marmalade for presents, and to add a bit of colour and cheer just before decanting, I stir through a couple of cups of dried cranberries. They look like Christmas jewels.

English breakfast tea

Breakfast tea, as such, was developed by a Scottish tea master named Drysdale. He identified the need for a strong brew to accompany the hearty cooked breakfast of the time (consisting say of roast pork and bread or potatoes), and to distinguish it from 'Afternoon tea', which was taken in the afternoon with light finger food, as promulgated by Anna, Duchess of Bedford. (See chapter 4.)

Drysdale's blend was adopted by none other than Queen Victoria. She purchased it when in residence at Balmoral one summer and apparently became fanatical about it. London tea merchants of the day saw a perfect marketing opportunity and began blending their own variations on Drysdale's, adding the word 'English' to the name. Today it is most likely blended using Indian teas from Assam or Ceylon tea (now known as Sri Lankan) or even African tea from Kenya, but Drysdale made up his blends using black teas from China such as *Keemun*, which were very popular at that time.

Tea blends

Just as in the eighteenth century tea companies today make up their own house blends, many of which literally become trade secrets. Some teas are named for the time when best drunk, others for their point of origin and others for their connection to people in history such as Earl Grey.

Earl Grey Tea

It is believed that this tea was named after Charles Grey, the 2nd Earl Grey, and Prime Minister of Britain from 1830 to 1834.

There is a myth that the Earl was given the recipe in gratitude by a visiting Chinese mandarin whose son the Earl had rescued from drowning. It is the second most popular tea in Britain today and is a blend of bergamot, Indian and Ceylon (Sri Lankan) teas. Bergamot is an essential oil that comes from a pear-shaped orange that grows on a *Citrus aurantium bergamia* tree.

Drysdale lived in an era when breakfast was a very hefty affair. Today's wisdom holds that we should breakfast like kings, lunch like princes and sup like paupers. This is a great prescription and might lead to your having something further to your marmalade and toast for breakfast. An egg, perhaps?

How to boil the perfect breakfast egg to go with your choice of breakfast tea

Including the 'how to' with regards to boiling an egg may seem rather needless, but I have noted it down in case there are any first-timers. My father for instance once tried boiling an egg and only that once. He had no idea water was involved in the process. So, for all those egg-boiling novices out there, here is an outline of what to do. In my view 4½ minutes make the egg's consistency perfect. Serves 1

Ingredients:

1 egg (2 if appetite large)
salt and pepper
1–2 slices favourite bread
butter

Method:

Bring a saucepan of water to the boil and carefully introduce your egg, taking care not to let it crash on the base of the pan. Boil gently for 4½ minutes for a not-too-runny yolk (my preference).

While the egg is boiling, toast and then generously butter sliced bread. Cut buttered toast into finger-sized strips, slender enough to dip into the 4½-minute boiled egg. Alternatively, for something a bit less orthodox, the following recipe offers eggs with prosciutto and spinach.

Eggs coddled with spinach and prosciutto
Serves 4

Ingredients:
8 slices prosciutto
2 cups baby spinach leaves, blanched
4 eggs
$^{1}/_{3}$ cup grated parmesan
sea salt and black pepper

Method:
Place two slices of prosciutto in each of four buttered ramekin dishes.

Divide blanched spinach between the four ramekins.

Crack one egg into each ramekin and top with ¼ of the grated parmesan, fresh sea salt and ground black pepper.

Bake in a bain-marie in a 180°C oven for 10 minutes, or less according to your taste in eggs.

Blueberry buttermilk pancakes
Serves 4

Ingredients:
2 eggs
2 cups buttermilk
60g unsalted butter, melted
¼ cup castor sugar
2 cups plain flour, sifted
½ tsp salt
3 tbsp baking powder
1 cup fresh (or frozen blueberries)

Method:

Place eggs, buttermilk and melted butter in a large bowl and beat until combined.

Add sugar, flour, salt and baking powder and gently fold through until just combined.

Heat a large, heavy-based frying pan over a medium heat and add a knob of butter to grease it.

Add a few tablespoons of the mixture to the pan, aiming to make say three pancakes at a time, of approximately 10cm diameter.

Sprinkle blueberries over each pancake and cook until bubbles appear on the surface and the underside has begun to turn golden in colour, about 2–3 minutes.

Turn and cook for another 2–3 minutes until cooked through and golden.

TIP Buttermilk, by the way, is also absolutely delicious drunk straight out of the carton, just like a yoghurt-based milkshake or smoothie.

An Indian breakfast

Meanwhile taking a wider view, were you to wake up in India, chances are that you would have a cup or two of chai to get going in the morning. (Actually, my quirk is to drink it before going to bed as it really promises a restful night's sleep, but right now it is breakfast time.)

Chai

Chai has been an Indian tradition for centuries and centuries. It is a brew of black tea with a blend of spices, typically cinnamon, ginger, nutmeg, cloves, cardamom and pepper (although the recipe varies from region to region). It is consumed at all times of the day, and is customarily the first thing offered to visitors. So prevalent is the consumption of chai throughout India that baristas, known as *chaiwallahs*, can be found on almost every street corner. These *chaiwallahs* are a mainstay of the community, and their stands are often a source of local news and gossip just like our cafés.

Serves 1

Ingredients:

1–2 cardamom pods
1 cinnamon stick
1 cup milk
1½ tbsp sugar
2 tsp Indian tea leaves such as
Darjeeling or Assam

Method:

Grind the spices with a mortar and pestle.

Place ground spices into a saucepan and add 1 cup each of cold water and milk, and the sugar.

Cook over a low heat for 2 minutes. Add the tea leaves and simmer for a further few minutes and that's it.

If you are not partial to milk you can just as easily make this up with soya milk or water. Also, if you like the flavour of cloves, add them too.

A delicious snack of middle-eastern origin to go with your chai early or mid-morning is Halva.

Halva

Serves 6–8

Ingredients:

100g ghee or unsalted butter
100g fine semolina
100g ground almonds
100g sugar
½ tsp ground nutmeg
300ml full cream milk
25g raw cashews, chopped

Method:

Grease a large plate and set aside.

Melt ghee or butter over a low heat until golden brown (6–7 minutes) stirring continuously.

Add semolina, almonds, sugar and nutmeg. Stir and mix thoroughly.

Add milk and mix, stirring until the mixture thickens and stops sticking to the bottom and sides of the pan.

Put the mixture onto your greased plate and spread it evenly to about 2cm thickness. Use the back of a spoon that has been lightly greased to do this effectively.

23

Then use a knife to press the sides inwards forming a large square. Sprinkle chopped cashews evenly on top and using the palm of your hand press them gently in.

Allow the mixture to cool and cut into 2½ cm squares.

Breakfast in Hong Kong and silk stocking tea

Were you in Hong Kong, you might be sipping on some exotic 'pantyhose tea' at the start of the day. This so-called Hong Kong milk tea is also known as 'silk stocking tea' because it is often brewed in a large tea sock that resembles pantyhose. It has a smooth, creamy texture and seductive full, sweet, flavour just like chai.
Serves up to 6

Ingredients:
1 cup water
2 tbsp black tea leaves
(preferably a bold Ceylon tea)
400ml sweetened condensed milk,
or evaporated milk, (adding
sugar to taste)

Method:
Combine water and tea leaves in a small saucepan over medium heat.

Bring to a gentle boil and then reduce heat and simmer for 3 minutes.

Remove from heat. Stir in sweetened, condensed (or evaporated) milk. Return to heat.

Bring back to boil. Simmer for 3 more minutes.

Strain and serve hot or for something entirely different you can serve your silk stocking tea chilled over ice in a martini glass. (This chilled version makes me nostalgic for Brandy Alexander or Bailey's Irish Cream.)

Chapter 2

Morning tea, 'smoko' and billy tea

Morning tea or 'smoko', as it is fondly known in Australia, is that much awaited moment when you can take a break; whether you have been teaching kindergarten kids, writing political manifestos, shearing sheep or filling in the pot holes created by the latest flood. It may be taken any old how, and is definitely improved by a biscuit or muffin. Most importantly morning tea is an opportunity to pause, re-group and re-charge.

Smoko

'Smoko' has its origins in rural Australia when stockmen, jackeroos and roustabouts took a pause from their work, had a 'cuppa' and a 'bit of sustenance'. Out in the bush that bit of sustenance would likely have been some damper. Colonial stockmen developed the technique of making damper from sheer necessity. Often away from home for weeks with just a campfire to cook on and the only provision being flour, it became their staple. Originally made with flour and water and a good pinch of salt, it was kneaded, shaped into a round, and baked in the ashes of the campfire or an open fireplace. With a bit of luck, though not always, it was eaten with pieces of fried dried meat, sometimes spread with golden syrup, but always with billy tea or maybe a swig of rum!

The billy

A billy is literally a cylindrical container for holding liquids, sometimes enamelled, and it usually has a lid. However it can be any container for boiling water and making tea, and is often makeshift. One speaks of boiling the billy, which may well come from the Scottish term to *bally* a milk-pail. The Billy Tea brand has been marketed in Australia since 1888, as 'a genuine campfire brew'. I certainly vouch for how delicious it is, especially when prepared out of doors.

Bush damper

Makes one small round loaf

Ingredients:

   3 cups of self-raising flour
   ½ tsp salt (optional)
   3 tbsp butter
   ½ cup milk
   ½ cup water

Method:

Sift flour and salt into a bowl and rub in the butter until the mixture resembles fine crumbs.

Make a well in the centre, add the combined milk and water, stir with a knife until dough leaves the sides of the bowl.

Gently knead on a lightly floured surface and then shape into a round, put on a greased oven tray.

Pat into a round of 15–16cm diameter.

With a sharp knife, cut two slits across the dough in the form of a cross, approximately 1cm deep.

Brush the top of the dough with milk. Sift a little extra flour over the dough.

Bake in a hot oven for 10 minutes, or until golden brown.

Reduce the heat to moderate and bake for another 20 minutes.

(Best eaten the day it is made.)

Billy tea

Should you be fortunate enough to be near a campfire at this point in the day, and have a billy handy, you can have the greatest of pleasure preparing yourself some 'billy tea'. All it takes is some water, tea leaves and a stick. Once you have simmered your leaves for five or so minutes, stirring occasionally, you remove the can from the heat, place it on the ground, tap it with your stick, causing the leaves to congregate at the bottom of the can, and your tea is ready to go.

ANZAC biscuits

These traditional biscuits were first baked by Australian wives and mothers during World War I, packed in food parcels, and sent to their menfolk in the trenches. They are hard to pass up, both for their flavour and for their history.

Makes about 24

Ingredients:

1 cup plain flour
²/₃ cup sugar
1 cup rolled oats
1 cup desiccated coconut
125g unsalted butter
¼ cup golden syrup
½ tsp bicarbonate of soda
1 tbsp boiling water

Method:

Preheat the oven to 180°C and line a 32x28cm tray with baking paper.

Sift the flour and sugar together in a large bowl.

Add oats and coconut to the flour and form a well in the centre.

Melt the butter and golden syrup together.

Dissolve bicarbonate of soda in water in a cup and add to the butter mixture which will then foam up.

Add this to the dry ingredients and stir, using a wooden spoon, until well mixed.

Drop one level tablespoon at a time of the mixture onto the prepared tray and use fingers to gently flatten, leaving space for expansion.

Bake for 10–15 minutes until just browned.

Remove from the oven and cool on a wire rack.

Crunchy muesli bars (an ideal snack for school children's lunch boxes)

Makes 16–20

Ingredients:

¾ cup dried apricots cut into small pieces (scissors are handy for this)
¼ cup sultanas
4 cups rice bubbles
½ cup icing sugar, sifted
1 cup full cream milk powder
¼ cup toasted sesame seeds
250g Copha, melted and slightly cooled

Method:

Grease and line 30x20cm baking tin. Combine all ingredients. Press mixture into tin and refrigerate until firm — best overnight.

Remove from tin and cut into bars.

Pumpkin scones
(for a savoury morning tea)

Makes 12–16

Ingredients:

250g pumpkin (steamed,
or roasted till soft — about 15
minutes in a moderate oven
— and allowed to cool)
2 cups sifted self-raising flour
1 egg yolk
½ cup castor sugar
1 tbsp butter

Method:

Mash all the ingredients together and knead the mixture to form a dough: it should be sticky to the touch.

Roll out flat and cut out rounds using the rim of a glass or cup, dipped in flour.

Place scones on a greased oven tray, and bake in a 180°C oven for 15 minutes.

Scones should sound hollow when tapped.

TIP For taller scones, bake in a muffin tray.

Brownies

For those with a sweet tooth, these are excellent pick-me-ups with your favourite mid-morning cuppa. Mine would be Russian Caravan at this point in the day. (At the end of this chapter I have included a bit of background on Russian tea and caravans.)

Makes 12

Ingredients:

125g unsweetened chocolate
250g unsalted butter
200g castor sugar
4 eggs
vanilla to taste
95–100g plain flour

Method:

Melt chocolate in top of double boiler over hot water until just melted.

Cover (once melted) and set aside.

In a medium bowl, cream butter and sugar.

Add eggs one at a time, beating well after each addition.

Stir the melted chocolate and vanilla into the egg mixture.

Sift the flour and salt into the chocolate mixture and stir gently but be careful not to over mix.

Pour into a buttered 23x33cm pan. (Important to be fussy about size of pan otherwise your brownies may not be their best).

Bake in 175° oven for 25–30 minutes until the centre bounces back.

Really take care not to over-bake.

Cool to warm before cutting into squares.

Optional: Dust with icing sugar.

Walnut brownies
Makes 16

Ingredients:
200g dark cooking chocolate
125g butter
½ cup brown sugar
3 eggs, lightly beaten
¾ cup self-raising flour
⅓ cup milk
¾ cup chopped walnuts

Method:
Preheat the oven to 180°C.

Break chocolate into small pieces.

Chop butter and add it to the chocolate.

On a low heat on the stove gently heat butter and chocolate in a medium-sized saucepan, melting it without it bubbling.

Remove from the heat and carefully fold in the brown sugar.

Add eggs, stirring carefully.

Slowly sift in the flour and fold it into the mixture.

Add milk, mixing it in completely.

Add chopped walnuts.

Pour the mixture into a greased medium-sized baking tray lined with baking paper and bake for about 25 minutes.

Remove from the oven and turn onto a wire rack until cool and cut into squares.

Optional: Dust with icing sugar.

Tales of samovars and fruity brews

Since its introduction to Russia, tea drinking has become embedded in Russian culture and the samovar (a truly elaborate but elegant tea kettle) is its centrepiece. Traditionally Russians combined two or even three teas together in their brews. They might have selected dark loose black tea from India (Assam for example), or a Chinese black tea such as *Keemun*, to make up a blend, as prepared in the samovar.

Russian caravan tea

An enduring favourite of mine, this Chinese black tea truly does owe its addictive smoky quality to its early experience of sitting alongside the campfire. In the seventeenth century merchants would transport their tea from China to Russia in caravans of camels, a journey requiring upwards of 18 months, ample time for the tea to fully absorb that glorious smoky aroma. It is traditionally a blend of *Keemun* and *Lapsang Souchong*.

A Queen's influence

It was Queen Victoria who, after visiting one of her daughters in Russia, introduced the English to the Russian custom of adding lemon to their tea. Before that the English only ever took milk with their tea.

Russian tea prepared in a samovar

A large quantity of tea leaves are placed in the small pot on the top of the samovar and covered with boiling water kept in the large centre section of the samovar. The resulting dark brew is known as *zavarka*. The *zavarka* is the essence of the drink and once brewed is literally on tap for the rest of the day, and even the following morning. A small amount of *zavarka* is poured into a cup and topped up with boiling water as required according to your preference.

Alternative Russian brew

Serves 12 or more

If you happen not to have a samovar to hand, why not try this simple saucepan-friendly recipe for a Russian-styled brew. It could even be prepared in the fashion of a billy-styled tea, and it would work brilliantly on a camping trip provided you remember to take along all the ingredients.

Ingredients:

1 cup of white sugar
8 cloves
grated rind of one medium orange
juice from 4 oranges
juice from 1 lemon
water, say 5 cups + 8 cups
1 tbsp of loose black tea leaves

Method:

Put the sugar, orange rind, cloves and the five cups of water into a saucepan and boil for 5 minutes.

Strain and allow it to cool.

Boil eight cups of water and add loose black tea leaves.

Steep for 3–4 minutes and strain.

Add spiced sugar-water and sip away.

Sbiten

Serves 12 or more

Historically a hot drink favoured by the Russians is *sbiten*. It pre-dates tea-drinking as we know it and is actually leaf-free. It is still enjoyed in Russia today. It's an ideal winter warmer and would also be great when out camping.

Ingredients:

3L water
1 cup honey
1 tsp each: cinnamon,
cloves and mint
1 cup berries or cranberry juice

Method:

Bring water to the boil.
Dissolve honey in the hot water.
Add spices, then the berries or
cranberry juice.
Allow it to simmer for half an hour.
Strain off herbs and fruit and it's
ready to go.

Naturally, you may want to have a
Russian teacake recipe to go with this
brew — but it's not easy to bake
in a campfire.

Russian teacakes
**(I have noticed these in Sydney
delicatessens, but how much better
to make your own.)**
Makes 35 or so

Ingredients:

240g soft butter
½ cup icing sugar
1 tsp of vanilla extract
2¼ cups plain flour
¼ tsp salt
¾ cup of chopped walnuts
1/3 cup of icing sugar for decoration

Method:

Combine the butter and icing sugar
in a mixing bowl.
Add the vanilla extract and mix
it in well.
Gradually add flour and salt to the
mixture, and beat in.
Add nuts and roll the dough
into a ball.
Cover it and chill it in the fridge for
a couple of hours.

Heat the oven to 200°C.

The dough will have become seriously hard, so you will need a spoon to help you take small pieces of it to squeeze into little balls.

Place them in the oven on a greased tray and bake for 10 minutes.

To decorate:

Put $1/3$ cup of icing sugar in a bowl and dunk the teacakes in it while still warm. Allow the sugar to melt into the balls. Put them on a serving plate and they are ready to go.

Chapter 3

How about a picnic?

Some of my happiest childhood memories have to do with picnics. The picnic may have been a simple affair on the lawn at home, but more likely at a point-to-point, the English steeple-chasing cousin of Australian picnic races.

Looking back the seeming simplicity of a picnic lay in the mastery of one's mother, and my mother was a wonderful creator of picnic fare. From my adult perspective I see now how much work was actually entailed to give us all easy and portable feasts. It must have been, and still can be, challenging and I am pretty sure we did not have Tupperware then. I cannot imagine anyone needs guidance on what they want on their picnic; for me these days it's about ensuring I have a comfortable chair! However after planning what tea to put in my flask I include a recipe for a particularly portable smoked tea salad dressing I have recently come across; it is thick (like a traditional rich French dressing) so travels well. In fact I keep it on standing order in my refrigerator. And I include a few modest suggestions for sandwiches.

Orange pekoe

Orange pekoe is described by the industry as a basic medium-grade black tea. I describe it as mellow and calming and refreshing. When I have had a few cups of strong tea early in the day I am keen for a tea that is less assertive. Orange pekoe fits the bill perfectly. In North America the term refers to any generic black tea (see Aunt Lucile's iced tea) although some merchants will define it to their customers as a specific variety. For me it is about the impact and the outcome. Orange pekoe never over stimulates. It just nurtures. And not being too strong in flavour I think it an ideal component in a picnic hamper.

Darjeeling

Darjeeling would be another contender. Darjeeling has been called 'the champagne of teas' as it is light and delicate. However Darjeeling's many tea estates (also known as tea gardens) produce a variety of teas with different characteristics. As its flavour is not overwhelming I believe it is also a worthy picnic contender.

Smoked tea vinaigrette
Makes 1 cup

Ingredients:

2 tsp Lapsang Souchong
or a 'smoky' tea in leaf form
1 tsp mustard powder
or 2 tsp Dijon mustard
$^1/_3$ cup virgin olive oil
$^1/_3$ cup sunflower oil
¼ cup white wine vinegar
½ tsp salt

Method:

Grind tea with mortar and pestle.

Gradually add the olive oil drip by drip into the mustard beating gently with a fork or whisk until it becomes an emulsion.

Gradually add sunflower oil, then vinegar and salt.

Add ground, smoked tea leaves.

Leave for six or so hours for flavours to infuse.

Season to taste.

This is a perfect portable dressing for your perfect and portable salad. This salad may carry the name of 'Chef's' (being you) or Cobb (if you are in America). Basically it is just all those ingredients you like in a salad, and might on this occasion include for your picnic.

Shankleesh
Shankleesh is a Lebanese cheese similar to feta, delicious however very pungent-smelling.

Ingredients:

3–4 pieces Shankleesh
1 red onion
2 Lebanese cucumbers
3 tomatoes
1 small bunch mint
1 cup black pitted olives
juice ½ lemon
$^1/_3$ cup olive oil
black pepper

Method:

Finely slice onion and cucumbers and toss together in a bowl.

Quarter tomatoes and add to bowl.

Tear mint leaves from stalks and add.

Add olives.

Toss and then add *Shankleesh*, lemon juice and olive oil.

Sandwich combinations

It's about bread (and there is an amazing array of it available these days), some type of spread (as a sealer) and whatever you love in between.

Ant, my husband, loves triple-decker sandwiches. He enjoys the look of three bread types rendered together to make a mini meal. Some rye, white and wholemeal for example can be very effective, with something delicious holding the trio of breads together. A little vegetable and a little protein go a long way and I often use pesto as a spread or olive tapenade. Here are a couple of ideas (ancient and modern) but truly I think everyone should be their own architect in this department.

• *Grilled or smoked chicken with marinated vegetables and a thin slice of brie*

• *Bocconcini, prosciutto, pesto and your favourite bit of green leaf*
• *Egg, mayonnaise, capers, crispy cos lettuce and lots of salt and pepper*
• *Smoked salmon (refreshed with a squeeze of lemon) and crème fraîche jazzed up with some rocket or other herbs*
• *Ham off-the-bone with your favourite cheese, some tomato, and a bit of pickle. (It's hard to go past this one)*
• *Lamb's brains (poached in milk) with lettuce and walnuts. (An old fashioned treat for my husband although not my cup of tea!)*

Cucumber sandwiches present something altogether daintier and belong in a class of their own. For me they speak of afternoon tea, of distinction and refinement.

39

Chapter 4

Afternoon tea,
high tea or 'arvo' tea

Anna Maria Russell, the seventh Duchess of Bedford, is credited with initiating the practice of 'afternoon tea' in the early 1800s as the perfect solution to her between-meal hunger pangs. Afternoon tea presented itself as a magnificent opportunity for socialising and showing off silverware, porcelain and tea and of course all its accoutrements: caddies, caddy spoons, sugar bowls, silver platters and not least of all teapots.

'I went to the Duchess for tea
It was just as I thought it would be
Her rumblings abdominal
Were simply phenomenal
And everyone thought it was me!'
Anon

Weather permitting afternoon tea may have been taken out of doors in an open-air tea garden. One of the most famous was the Ranelagh Gardens in Chelsea which boasted a rotunda designed after the Pantheon in Rome. Entry to the gardens was two shillings and six pence (about 20c). If you were seriously lucky you might have heard Mozart playing there, which he did on occasion for the Duke of Cumberland. You may have attended a tea dance even.

High tea

The term 'high tea' is actually owed to Britain's nineteenth century working class, who transformed afternoon tea into their primary evening meal, when much heartier fare was served such as meats, cakes, bread and pies. (This was in stark contrast to the dainty finger food enjoyed by society's upper classes.)

'High' tea also takes its reference from the table at which working people took their tea. It was tall by contrast to the low, delicate tables at which the gentry took their lighter, more formal 'afternoon' tea.

'High tea' also refers in many households to the meal young children have at the end of their day, aka 'nursery tea'.

Arvo tea

'Arvo' tea is Australian shorthand for afternoon tea, and what better to go with it than an English scone known as a biscuit in America?

Scones

Scones are an English classic and the tea that you may consider serving with them is Prince of Wales tea.

Prince of Wales tea

Prince of Wales tea is a blend of Chinese black teas. The blend was originally devised for Edward, Prince of Wales.

Scones with clotted cream and jam
Makes 8–10

Ingredients:

2 cups self-raising flour
large pinch salt
2 tbsp castor sugar
¼ cup (85g) diced butter
150ml milk
1 egg, beaten (or milk)
for brushing on dough

Method:

Heat the oven to 220°C, placing baking tray in it to warm up.

Sift flour and salt together.

Stir in sugar and then rub in butter until it resembles breadcrumbs.

Make a well in the centre and stir in milk so as to make a soft, not sticky, mixture.

Knead for a few moments and then gently roll it out to about 2cm depth on a lightly floured surface.

Use a 5cm cutter to cut out 8–10 circles.

(A neat alternative is to cut scones into triangles using a sharp, reliable knife.)

Bake near the top of the oven for about 8–10 minutes until well risen and golden.

Cool a little on a wire rack, but these are at their best served warm with strawberry jam and clotted cream.

Hassle-free scones

I have just been given this amazing and surprisingly straightforward Queensland recipe for scones by a Scottish school-friend with whom I attended an English boarding school. There are only three ingredients and provided you don't over-knead the dough, Nicky tells me, it's fail-safe. (And it's so simple that you could take the ingredients with you for a baking session on a camping trip, or a picnic.) Makes 10–12

Ingredients:
3 cups self-raising flour
1 cup pouring cream
1 cup lemonade

Method:
Pop all ingredients straight into a bowl and stir gently. (It is important not to over-stir.)

Place on counter, roll out and cut out scones as above.

Pop onto heated tray into hot oven as before (220°C) for approximately 10 minutes and you will be in possession of perfect hassle-free scones.

Fruit scones
Add ⅓ cup currants, sultanas, raisins, chopped dates or figs, or a combination of some or all of the above to the basic scone mixture, omitting the sugar component. (A particularly good combination is cranberry together with a bit of lemon rind.)

Apple and honey scones
After adding the butter, add two grated, peeled and cored apples.

Use 3–4 tbsp honey and 3–5 tbsp milk to bind the mixture into a dough.

½ tsp ground cinnamon is an essential in this version.

Strawberry jam, for those interested in DIY jam
Makes 8 to 10 jars depending on their sizes

Ingredients:
1.6kg strawberries
2 tbsp lemon juice
1.5kg sugar

Method:

Gently simmer strawberries and lemon juice for about 30 minutes until good and soft.

Add sugar, allow it all to dissolve and boil rapidly until 'setting point'. (Drop a little onto a cool plate, cool slightly and push gently with a finger. If the surface wrinkles, the jam is ready.)

This may take up to an hour but never wander far.

Once the jam has reached this point, turn off the heat, allow the jam to cool for 10–15 minutes and then decant into sterilised jars (approximately 8–10) and seal.

Choccie-bicky cake

I am not quite sure what the Duchess of Bedford may have enjoyed, but for me this was a boarding school treat. It really cheered up afternoon tea, when the ingredients were available. It is also a great recipe for young chefs as minimal assistance is required, and no baking. Makes enough for 24

Ingredients:

24 plain sweet biscuits, milk arrowroot are ideal
250g cream cheese, at room temperature
250g unsalted butter, at room temperature
¾ cup castor sugar
¾ cup sifted cocoa powder
1 tsp vanilla essence
hundreds and thousands, or favourite sweets

Method:

Line the base of a lightly greased 23cm square cake tin with baking paper.

Arrange 12 sweet biscuits evenly across the base.

Combine cream cheese, butter, sugar, cocoa and vanilla essence and beat until smooth.

Spread half the cream mixture across the biscuits and then arrange the next 12 biscuits on top before spreading the remaining mixture across the top of them.

Decorate however you please; otherwise, plain can be perfectly delicious.

Cool in a refrigerator for a minimum of three hours, preferably overnight.

TIP To serve, cut into squares, using a hot dry knife.

Auntie Goy's gingerbread
Serves 10–12

Ingredients:
1 cup sugar
250g softened butter
1 egg
½ cup golden syrup
1 cup milk
2 cups plain flour
1 tsp baking powder
1 tsp cinnamon
2 tsp all spice
3 tsp ground ginger

Method:
Cream together the butter and sugar.

Add all the remaining ingredients and beat thoroughly.

Pour into a prepared 14x24cm loaf tin.

Bake in a moderate oven at 175°C for approximately 45 minutes.

You may turn it onto a wire rack to cool although you may prefer to serve it warm straight from the oven and spread thickly with butter.

Irish breakfast tea
I like to imagine that my husband's Auntie Goy might have served Irish breakfast tea with her gingerbread in tribute to her Irish forebears. Like English breakfast tea, Irish breakfast tea is a blend of several black teas (often from Assam) but is rather more robust. Unsurprisingly in Ireland, it is not referred to as 'Irish breakfast tea', just good old breakfast tea. It is served strong and customarily with milk and is another of my favourites.

Brazil and hazelnut bread
Serves 8–10

Ingredients:
5 egg whites
pinch salt
170g castor sugar
170g plain flour
1 tsp cinnamon
155g mixed Brazil and hazelnuts
(coarsely chopped)

Method:
Beat the egg whites with salt until stiff.

Gradually add sugar, beating well after each addition.

Sift the plain flour and cinnamon and fold it in a spoonful at a time.

Fold in the chopped nuts.

Spoon the mixture into a glazed, lined, greased 14x24cm loaf tin.

Bake in a moderate oven at 175°C, for approximately 45 minutes.

Cool in the tin.

Alternatively serve thinly sliced and warm from the oven.

Spread thickly with butter for extra indulgence.

Raspberry and white chocolate muffins
Makes approximately 12

Ingredients:
170g sugar
2 eggs
200g butter, softened
200g sifted self-raising flour
80ml milk
½ cup frozen raspberries (and extra for muffin tops)
¼ cup white chocolate chips (and extra for muffin tops)

Method:
Whisk the sugar and eggs together until thick.

Add the butter, flour and then the milk.

Throw in raspberries and chocolate chips and stir gently to combine.

Spoon into muffin tins, pressing extra raspberries and chocolate chips onto muffin tops.

Bake in a moderate oven 180°C for 30 minutes or until golden brown.

Flapjacks with banana cream and strawberries

Flapjack is an English word, elsewhere these little treats are also known as pikelets or griddlecakes. I remember toasting them in front of the fire as a child while enjoying my first tea-drinking experience. It was simply 'China' tea with lots of milk and sugar. I can still taste the magic.
Makes approximately 18–20

Ingredients:

2 cups self-raising flour
pinch salt
1/3 cup sugar
1 egg
2/3 cup milk
1 tsp white vinegar
1 tsp melted butter

Method:

Combine milk and vinegar in a bowl and set aside.

Sift flour and salt, and stir in the sugar.

Form a well in the centre, and break the egg into the middle.

Slowly stir the egg in gathering flour into the centre and then gradually add the milk, stirring until the batter is fairly thick.

Heat a heavy-based frying pan and brush the surface with a little melted butter.

Drop tablespoons of batter into the pan ensuring they are not too close.

Once bubbles appear on the surface, flip over and cook on other side for 1–2 minutes, they should be a light golden brown.

Wipe the pan with a paper towel, brush the surface with melted butter, and continue to cook spoonfuls of batter until you have a plateful of flapjacks.

47

Banana cream and strawberries

Ingredients:
2 ripe bananas
juice of ½ lemon
300ml cream
3 punnets strawberries

Method:
Process bananas with lemon juice in a blender.

Whip cream until stiff.

Fold in banana purée and then chill for a while.

Wash strawberries, hull and slice thickly.

When ready to serve, place a dollop of cream on top of the flapjacks and dress with sliced strawberries.

Alternatively, serve flapjacks with:

Fresh squeeze of lemon juice and white sugar; jam and whipped or clotted cream; butter and maple syrup; or at breakfast time maple syrup and bacon!

Moll's apricot biscuits
Makes 18–20

Ingredients:
1 large tbsp softened butter
½ cup sugar
1½ cups self-raising flour, sifted
apricot jam

Method:
Preheat the oven to 180°C.

Cream together the butter and sugar until light and fluffy.

Fold in sifted flour and mix well.

Take walnut-sized pieces (1tsp) of the mixture and roll into balls and place into greased patty tins or a flat tray.

Make a depression in each ball and fill with apricot jam.

Bake for 15 minutes until light brown.

Allow them to cool before removing them.

Jenny's short biscuits
Makes 18–20

Ingredients:
185g softened butter
½ cup sifted icing sugar
1½ cup sifted self-raising flour
2 dessertspoons custard powder
pinch salt

Method:
Pre-heat oven to 180°C.

Cream together butter and icing sugar.

Add self-raising flour, custard powder and salt.

Roll into balls and press flat with a fork.

Bake for 15 minutes.

Remove from oven cool and tip onto platter to serve.

Speedy green afternoon teacake

I recently had the privilege of sipping tea with my friend Roly, in a beautiful teahouse, local to where I live and we were slipped, most generously as it turns out, by our tea host, his recipe for a 'speedy green afternoon teacake'. Without disclosing which teahouse we were in I shall share the speedy part of the exchange. In brief the method is as follows:

Serves 10–12

Ingredients:
1 supermarket bought cake mix for a standard teacake
1 tsp matcha green tea
*(*Matcha *is Japanese green tea in fine powder form: one of the most popular green teas in Japan today. It is highly significant in Japanese culture as it is served as part of the Japanese Tea Ceremony (described in chapter 9). It can be purchased*

from online tea stores if it is not kept in your local Asian supermarket.)

Method:

Follow all directions on pack. Just prior to baking mix in 1 tsp *matcha*.

Hey presto, your teacake is green! (A mellow natural mossy green, not vivid.) Which takes me back to my earlier point about tea and its magic. I have been thinking that you could add *matcha* to whipped cream to lend it some colour or any variety of foodstuffs. You could possibly even colour up a white sauce for fish.

High tea

The following recipes are a little more robust, and well suited to 'high tea' or supper.

Crabcakes

I have included this recipe because, always given to nostalgia, I associate a specific afternoon tea involving our family with some delicious crabcakes eaten many years ago at Bunchrew, a wonderful old house near Inverness in Scotland that purported to be haunted. Serves 5–6

Ingredients:

400g crabmeat, well-drained
1¼ cups breadcrumbs
½ onion, finely diced
2 tbsp finely chopped coriander
3 finely diced shallots
2 finely diced small red chillies
juice ½ lime
1 egg, beaten
salt and pepper to taste
1–2 cups breadcrumbs for coating
olive oil for frying

Method:

Combine all the ingredients and press them all together to form a soft mixture.

(Add breadcrumbs if the mixture is too soggy).

Form into small 'cakes'.

Coat cakes lightly with breadcrumbs.

Heat oil in a frying pan and cook

gently for approximately a minute on each side, or until light and golden.

Drain and serve with sour cream, tartar sauce or aioli, and a twist of lemon.

Salmon fishcakes

Cousins to the crabcakes, and just as delicious, albeit a little milder. They are ideal for nursery tea, high tea or supper.
Makes 8–10

Ingredients:

600g fresh salmon or ocean trout fillets, skinned and baked in a 180°C oven for 10 minutes
400g cooked and mashed potatoes
1 tsp Worcestershire sauce
1 tbsp tomato sauce
1 tsp Dijon mustard
1 tsp capers, rinsed and chopped
2 tsp grated lemon zest
2 tbsp fresh chopped parsley
sea salt and pepper
2 tbsp plain flour

2 eggs, beaten
1–2 cups fresh or dry breadcrumbs
1 tbsp butter
2 tbsp oil
1 lemon, quartered

Method:

Use a fork to gently break up baked fish and fold pieces carefully into mashed potato with Worcestershire sauce, tomato sauce, Dijon, capers, lemon zest, parsley and a generous amount of salt and pepper.

Form into 8 'cakes' (a pastry or biscuit cutter can help), and chill for 30 minutes in the fridge.

Dip cakes into flour, then beaten egg and finally the breadcrumbs, ensuring they are completely coated.

Heat butter and oil in a frying pan and cook cakes on one side until golden brown (only a couple of minutes), then turn and lightly cook the other side.

Drain on a kitchen towel and serve with lemon wedges, and as with crabcakes, sour cream, tartar sauce or aioli.

And while we are still looking at savoury options it would be remiss to overlook a vintage favourite for kids and grown up children:

Toad-in-the-hole

One of our daughters recently enjoyed this dish in an English boarding school where she worked during her gap year. It's a staple there, but it was also one in our Aussie household when our children were younger. The dish is essentially a pancake-style mix baked over sausages. I choose pork but any sausage would suit, even chorizo for something a bit sharper.
Serves 4

Ingredients:
1 cup plain flour
pinch salt
1 egg
300ml milk
1 tbsp Worcestershire sauce
8 sausages (or more depending on mouths to be fed)

Method:
Heat the oven to 220°C.

Sift the flour and salt into a large bowl and make a well in the centre.

Crack the egg and a little milk into the well.

Using a wire whisk gently draw the dry ingredients into the well.

When the mixture is smooth, slowly pour in the rest of the milk and the Worcestershire sauce whisking continually to make sure the batter does not grow lumpy.

Leave for 30 minutes to settle.

Prick the sausages and place them on a medium-sized baking tray.

Place into the oven for 5–10 minutes so some of their juice runs into the pan.

Give the batter a good stir and pour it over the sausages.

Bake for about 30 minutes until the batter rises to an inviting golden crisp.

Welsh rarebit

As a child I was uncertain about this dish, as it seemed 'rabbits' were involved and that did not sit too well with me. Once assured there was no rabbit content, and being a fervent lover of all things cheesy, it did not take long to develop a keen appetite for these delicious melted cheese snacks.

Serves 2

Ingredients:

2–4 slices of your favourite bread; (multigrain for me), although walnut bread can provide a fabulous contrast with the sharpness of the rarebit.
25g salted butter
25g plain flour
150ml milk, warmed
75g grated cheese (cheddar is best) and a little extra
Worcestershire sauce
paprika
1 tsp hot English mustard

Method:

Turn grill onto medium heat.

Toast your bread on both sides under the grill and set aside.

Melt butter in a pan, add flour and cook over low heat for 1–2 minutes making up a paste.

Slowly add warm milk to this, simmer and cook gently until thickened.

Stir in cheese, a splash of Worcestershire, a pinch of paprika and the mustard and then remove from heat.

Spread across your toasted bread and sprinkle with a bit of extra cheese and grill for a few moments more until the cheese bubbles golden.

Serve straight up or with a salad.

Chapter 5

An American take on tea

Iced tea has been consumed in
America for a hundred years or more
and its consumption is still on the rise.
Apparently more than 8.4 billion litres
of tea are imbibed each year, about
80 per cent of which (around 6.6 billion
litres is iced. This equates to an average
of nearly 24.6 litres per person per year.

In the cooler climes of England by contrast (and the measurement is in weight because now we are talking about tea leaves) on average 3.2 kilograms (7 pounds of tea) are brewed and drunk in an average year per person.

There are some significant and exotic variations on standard iced tea. Long Island iced tea is a stunner. This is a tea that looks like a tea but definitely isn't one. With its alcohol (a staggering five in the one cocktail) and sugar content, it is guaranteed to perk you up. Though too much might give you a sore head the following day.

Long Island iced tea
Serves 1

Ingredients:
15ml each vodka, gin, tequila, rum and triple sec
25ml sour mix or bitter lemon
splash of sugar syrup
5 cubs ice (or thereabouts)
top up coca cola
1 wedge lemon

Method:
Shake together all ingredients except cola and lemon wedge and pour over ice. Top up with cola and decorate with lemon wedge.

Aunt Lucile's iced tea
Aunt Lucile is my grandmother's sister.
Serves 20

Ingredients:
20 cups (5L) water
10 oranges
7 lemons
1 cup orange pekoe tea leaves
1 large bunch fresh mint
3 cups sugar

Method:
Bring water to boil in a large saucepan.
Squeeze all oranges and lemons.

Put their juice aside.

Place all their rinds into the large saucepan of boiling water.

Add tea leaves and mint and continue to boil gently for an hour.

Leave to cool.

Extract rinds having squeezed them tightly.

Strain tea leaves and mint, and place liquid tea into large pitcher or jug.

Add sugar and stir until dissolved.

Add squeezed juice to the tea and serve over ice.

Iced tea with a nip of Angostura's
Makes two litres

Ingredients:
3–4 tsp your favourite tea brewed for five minutes in say 6 cups of water, then cooled and chilled
2–3 tsp sugar (or sugar syrup)
1 lemon finely sliced
1–3 dashes Angostura 'aromatic' bitters
lots of ice

Method:
Once your tea is brewed, strained and chilled, put it in a large jug over a cupful or two of ice, sliced lemon or lime, and sugar.

Stir well, and add a shake or two of Angostura bitters.

Angel food cake
Not too far from the ubiquitous albeit delicious, pavlova.
This is an American classic often served in my childhood by my mother, who was raised in the south, naturally accompanied by Aunt Lucile's traditional iced tea. To bake an angel food cake you need a special tube pan. This is akin to a round cake tin but it has a central column making the finished product resemble a giant ring rather than a sphere (and is available in speciality cookware shops).
Serves 10

Ingredients:
1 cup plain flour

1½ cups sugar
12 egg whites
¾ tsp salt
1½ tsp cream of tartar
2 tsp grated lemon rind
½ tsp vanilla extract
berries to serve (optional)

Method:

Sift the flour and half the sugar into a bowl. Set aside.

In another bowl, beat the egg whites with salt until stiff.

Add the cream of tartar and continue to beat until very stiff.

Add the remaining sugar a spoonful at a time.

Fold through lemon rind, vanilla and flour mixture with a spatula.

Pour into a non-greased, thoroughly clean and dry 23–25cm angel food cake tin and bake at 190°C for 35–40 minutes or until cooked through when tested with a skewer.

Invert tin, and allow it to cool.

Run a knife around edges of the tin to release the cake; it should fall from the tin easily.

Serve with berries (and maybe a bit of whipped cream) and Aunt Lucile's traditional iced tea. (The recipe for this is earlier in this chapter.)

Pecan nut cookies

Pecans always make me think of America, and I find them irrististable. This is a simple and delicious recipe.
Makes approximately 20

Ingredients:

120g butter, softened
2 tbsp sugar
1 tsp vanilla essence
1 cup pecan nuts, ground finely in a processor
1 cup plain flour
pure icing sugar, sifted

Method:

Beat the butter, sugar and vanilla until creamy and then fold in the nuts and flour.

Form the mixture into small balls and bake on a greased tray in a preheated 150°C oven for 20 minutes.

Carefully roll the balls in icing sugar and bake for a further 15 minutes. And, to smarten them up why not pop a pecan nut on each at this stage.

The Boston Tea Party

This particular tea party (not the current one to which I pay absolutely no allegiance) took place on a bright, cold, moonlit evening in 1773. Sixty men, some of whom were dressed as Mohawks, boarded three tea-ships: the Dartmouth, the Eleanor and the Beaver, and emptied their entire collected cargo (342 chests of tea valued at £18,000) into Boston Harbour rendering it into a veritable teapot. In an effort to rescue the debt-ridden British East India Company, the British had granted it a monopoly on all tea exported to the colonies, an exemption on export tax and even a refund on duties owed on certain surplus quantities of tea in its possession. All this was arranged without any discussion with the colonists and it bypassed all the independent colonial shippers and

tea merchants. The colonists, sick of being trifled with, decided to remonstrate in a very emphatic manner.

This tea party became the first protest by the Sons of Liberty. It unified the colonists when their feelings about Britain had, for obvious reasons, taken a serious downward turn. King George and his ministers at Westminster were duly infuriated and diarists at the time noted that the House of Lords became like a seething cauldron of impotent rage but that it was not a mob that destroyed the cargo, rather sober, patriotic citizens encouraged by other patriotic citizens who had had enough. John Adams (soon to be America's second President) wrote that when the work was done, the streets of the town became as quiet as a Sabbath evening. All things were conducted with great order, decency and perfect submission to the government (British). However the British responded by passing more repressive laws and the American War of Independence soon erupted.

In Ireland meanwhile:

'Barm brack' or fruity tea bread. Barm brack (or bread) is as traditional a teacake as you may find. It is made using brewed tea. Do note that you need to start with this recipe one day ahead of time.

These quantities make three small loaves or one large and one small.

Barm brack and Hallowe'en

Irish folklore relates that a ring baked on Hallowe'en into a loaf of barm brack will foretell of imminent romance. He or she who receives the slice of bread with the ring in it will surely be the first to find love, true happiness and a proposal to wed the following year.

Ingredients:

450g sultanas
450g raisins
450g soft brown sugar
425ml brewed tea
450g plain flour
3 large eggs, beaten
1 tbsp baking soda
1 tbsp mixed spice
3 tbsp honey, warmed to glaze

Method:

Put the fruit, sugar and tea in a large mixing bowl and soak overnight.

The next day heat the oven to 170°C.

Butter and flour loaf tin(s).

Alternately add the flour and beaten eggs to the tea mixture.

Add baking powder and spice and mix well.

Pour the batter into prepared tins and smooth the surface(s).

Bake loaves for one and a half hours (an extra half hour for a large one).

Test with a skewer inserted into the centre to make sure they are cooked through.

Allow five minutes for cooling and then turn onto a wire rack.

When cold, gently warm honey and brush it over the tops of the loaves to glaze and then allow them to set.

Serve the bread in slices with plenty of butter.

Pursuing the Irish theme briefly, you may wish on the odd occasion (though only rarely) to turn your back on tea altogether and indulge in an old fashioned, uber-nostalgic, Irish coffee. Here's a reminder about how to prepare it. It is widely suggested in Ireland that this can be a good *start* to the day as well as a great way of wrapping one up. I for one am happy to take the challenge.

Irish coffee
Serves 1

Ingredients:
Coffee (prepared as you like it; sugared or not; the Irish way is hot and strong.)
50ml Irish whiskey
1 tbsp (or 2!) thick pouring cream

Method:
Warm your glass, goblet or mug.
Stir in sugar (if using) and coffee.
Add whiskey.
Stir again.
Hold a teaspoon (curved side up) across the rim of the glass, goblet or mug and pour the cream slowly over the back of the spoon so it floats on the coffee.

No more guidance required.

Chapter 6

Supper and tea-smoking your food

For me supper takes place any time from 6.00 or 7.00 in the evening. It is a meal that encompasses anything and everything. It may be pre-theatre, in front of the TV, in the garden, post-theatre, on the verandah, solo, with family, at the table or not, with friends, without friends.

It's exciting after years in the kitchen to be introduced to a novel way of cooking. That is where smoking food has recently played its part for me.

Smoking food is not only a great way of preparing food healthily but also of giving it a new twist. Foods smoked over tea leaves are absolutely delicious. The heady smoky flavour really speaks to the taste buds. The bergamot oil from Earl Grey tea for example gives a fantastic fragrance to food, and duck smoked with a *Lapsang Souchong* 'smoking' mixture is a great combo.

Step 1: The smoking envelope

Quantity industrial strength metal foil
¼ cup oolong, black or jasmine tea
¼ cup rice (preferably jasmine)
¼ cup light brown sugar
8 whole stars anise
1–2 sticks cinnamon (crushed)
¼ cup sliced onion
3–4 slices fine orange peel
1 tbsp sesame seeds (optional)

You can make up a smoking 'envelope' for use inside or out-of-doors. Inside you can use it in a wok with a wire tray, and outside you can place your envelope directly onto the coals, or over the burners, inside your barbecue.

Two important pointers:

– Ensure whatever food you are smoking is as dry as possible by patting it with a paper or tea towel. Dry food will absorb the smoky flavours more efficiently.

– Try to arrange your food so it is not directly over your smoking envelope. You are looking for an infusion not an inferno.

Here is a fantastic recipe for a smoky supper!

Tea-smoked salmon or ocean trout with Thai-style cucumber salad

Serves 6

Ingredients:

*6 salmon or ocean trout fillets
(skin on)*

Marinade:

*¼ cup soy sauce
1 tbsp sugar
2 tbsp finely grated orange zest
¼ tsp mild ground paprika*

Method:

Whisk together the soy sauce, sugar, orange zest and paprika.

Add salmon or ocean trout pieces and coat with the marinade.

Cover and keep cool in the refrigerator for an hour or so.

Thai-style cucumber salad

Ingredients:

*2 tbsp rice vinegar
1½ tbsp castor sugar
1 small red chilli (no seeds)
1 spring onion finely chopped
1 tbsp finely chopped
coriander leaves
2 tbsp grated ginger
2 cloves garlic, crushed
2 tsp canola oil
2 tsp fish sauce
1 telegraph cucumber or (3
Lebanese) cut into fine ribbons
with either a mandolin or
vegetable peeler*

Method for salad:

Dissolve sugar into vinegar in a bowl.

Finely slice the chilli, removing the seeds and add to the bowl along with the coriander, ginger, garlic, canola oil and fish sauce.

Place the cucumber into the marinade and set aside.

When your fish (below) is ready to serve, simply drain the marinade and arrange cucumber on serving plate alongside the smoked fish.

Tea-smoking the salmon or ocean trout

Put tea, rice, sugar, star anise, cinnamon, strips of orange peel, onion and sesame seeds into the centre of a sheet of industrial strength metal foil and fold loosely into a packet/envelope leaving it partially open. (Use a couple of sheets of foil if it is only lightweight quality.)

Warm up your barbecue (if using) and place your smoking packet gently on the coals or near its burners and replace barbecue lid. If you are using a wok indoors, line the wok with foil and warm it up. Then insert the smoking envelope at its base and a wire rack at its centre, not touching

the envelope, and then replace lid of the wok so the envelope can start to do its thing.

Leave your barbecue or wok for up to 10 minutes while the smoking packet works up its energy.

Meanwhile drain marinated salmon (or alternative fish) pieces, pat dry and gently brush with vegetable oil.

Place salmon pieces on grill plate either over coals or in wok — a little to the side of the envelope and close the lid.

Smoke for 3–5 minutes on each side until fish is done to your liking. (It is best to aim to only turn fish once.)

Leave the fish to settle for a few minutes before serving with Thai-style cucumber salad.

If you are feeding hungry hoards you may want some carbohydrates too. Here follows a recipe for roasted potatoes which takes its influence from India that can be baking in the oven while you are smoking your fish elsewhere.

65

Haveli spiced potatoes
Serves 6–8

Ingredients:
*1tsp each mustard seeds
and cumin seeds
½ tsp crushed red pepper
(or chilli) flakes
1 tsp salt
black pepper
¼ tsp turmeric
1kg potatoes cut into bite-size pieces
2 medium onions, chopped
3 tbsp olive oil*

Method:
Heat oven to 215°C.

In a mortar and pestle crush together the mustard seeds, cumin seeds, and red pepper flakes.

In a large bowl toss the seed and pepper mixture, salt, pepper, turmeric, potato, onion and olive oil.

Spread all of it on a baking tray and bake for about 45 minutes, tossing every 15 minutes, until potatoes are crunchy and onion is cooked through.

Tea-smoked chicken
Once you have prepared your chicken as below, you can serve it any which way. I like to put it with steamed spinach tossed in butter, garlic and parmesan. Alternatively you can let it cool and slice or shred it ready to pop into a salad.
Serves 4–6

Ingredients:
*4 chicken breasts (skin and
bone-free) or 8 thigh fillets
salt and pepper*

Smoking envelope
(prepared as above)

Ingredients for smoking envelope:
*¼ cup jasmine tea
¼ cup rice (preferably jasmine)
¼ cup light brown sugar
2 tbsp coriander seeds*

Method:

Pound chicken breasts, or fillets, between two sheets of cling-wrap until they are about 1.5cm thick.

Pat dry and season generously.

Loosely wrap tea, rice, sugar and coriander seeds in an envelope made from extra strength aluminium foil (as described above for smoked salmon or ocean trout).

If using a barbecue, place your envelope carefully on its glowing coals or burners and draw over the lid and leave for 10 or so minutes.

Alternatively if using a wok, place the envelope in the belly of the wok (lined with foil) on medium heat and cover. In actual fact you can put the smoking mixture directly onto the base of your foil-lined wok if you prefer. I have tried both methods and both work very well although the envelope helps to contain everything more efficiently.

Lightly brush chicken breasts with olive oil and arrange carefully either on barbecue grill or in your wok.

Smoke for approximately 5–7 minutes on each side (aiming to turn once only).

Remove from heat and either serve, or cool to room temperature in readiness for a salad.

I made the mistake of once letting the chicken sit in the wok once cooked. Not a great idea. It made the chicken disappointingly dry.

Sugary ideas to finesse your supper

Cardamom and ginger ice cream
Serves 6

Ingredients:

600ml thick whipping cream, whipped
10 gingernut biscuits, pulsed to resemble breadcrumbs in processor
20g cardamom pods, processed and kernels removed (or 2 tsp ground cardamom)
2 tbs orange marmalade

Method:
Fold this selection of ingredients together and freeze.

Gooey lemon syrup cake

There are many varieties of this recipe I have tried over the years: the most important element of them all is being generous with the syrup. The lemony zing makes the cake. It is a winner, accompanied of course by ice cream, cream, yogurt, whatever your preference.

Serves 8–10

Ingredients:
Cake:

125g butter, softened
250g castor sugar
2 large eggs
1 cup Greek yoghurt
1 tsp pure vanilla extract
zest 2 lemons

3 tbsp lemon juice
400g self-raising flour
½ tsp bicarbonate of soda

Syrup:
Frankly you can double these quantities and still want for more. The more gooey the cake, the better.

1 cup castor sugar
1 cup water
4 tbsp lemon juice
2 lemons, finely sliced

Method:
Preheat the oven to 180°C.

Grease and line a 23cm cake tin with a removable base.

Cream together the butter and sugar until light and fluffy.

Add eggs individually and continue to mix until the mixture is well blended.

Add the yoghurt, vanilla, lemon zest and juice and mix again.

Fold in the flour and bicarbonate of soda.

Smooth the mixture into the cake tin and bake for 45 minutes.

While it is baking, you can prepare the syrup.

Dissolve the sugar in water and lemon juice over low heat and then add the lemon slices to soften taking about 10 minutes.

Set aside.

When the cake is baked, use a skewer to puncture the surface with lots of holes: this is to allow the entire cake to be saturated with the syrup.

Pour all of syrup evenly across the cake.

Arrange the lemon slices as you wish.

Allow the cake to cool for a while, and then carefully lift it onto a serving plate. (Greek yoghurt is particularly good with this.)

Chocolate and almond cake

I will eat, cook or buy anything with almond meal in it. This delicious cake is a terrific accompaniment to any cup of tea, glass of wine, or sherry perhaps? Serves 8–10

Ingredients:
200g butter
4 eggs, separated
175g castor sugar
1 tsp vanilla extract
200g dark chocolate, either grated or melted and cooled
250g almond meal
icing sugar

Method:
Preheat the oven to 180°C.

Melt butter, set aside, and allow it to cool down.

Beat together egg yolks, sugar and vanilla extract until thick and pale.

Fold cooled melted butter, chocolate and almond meal into the mixture.

In a separate bowl whisk egg whites until soft peaks form and fold them into the chocolate mixture.

Spoon the mixture into a greased, lined 24cm cake tin and bake for 50–60 minutes until just firm.

Leave it in the tin to cool and then turn out.

Dust with icing sugar just before you serve.

Sauternes cake

This is great for a tea party with a dash of something different. (Alongside the pot of tea of your choice you might have some chilled champagne or sparkling wine.) But it is lovely at any time. It is rather like a giant friand and has that wonderful rich friand-texture, but it is not too heavy and it has a delicious citrus essence. I like it still warm from the oven but it is fabulous cold, too.
Serves 8–10

Ingredients:

4 whole eggs
¾ cup sugar
2–3 tbsp mixed grated orange and lemon peel
1 cup sifted flour
½ cup Sauternes (sherry as a substitute is absolutely fine and I am sure any white wine would also work)
½ cup extra virgin olive oil
4 additional egg whites

Method:

Separate the eggs and put in two separate bowls.

Cream yolks with sugar until light and fluffy.

Add the peel and then fold in the flour a little at a time.

Add the Sauternes and oil a little at a time.

In a clean bowl whip all the egg whites until firm.

Fold the whipped egg whites (8) into the cake mixture.

Pour the mixture into a lined 20cm spring form tin and bake at 180°C for 20 minutes, then lower the temperature to 160°C and continue baking for a further 20 minutes.

Turn off the oven and allow the cake to cool in it slowly for 10–20 minutes.

It will deflate a little.

Remove your cake from the oven, and from the tin, and allow it to cool down completely.

You can serve topped with icing sugar and fresh sliced or poached fruit such as peaches that might just have been marinated in a little Sauternes, (or a cold brewed fruity tea of your choice) and some cream or ice cream. Pouring some loosely whipped cream across the top is an idea.

Pineapple and cardamom upside-down cake

This is one of my favourite cakes and is perfect at any time. How about trying it in the evening with a cardamom cooler, listed in the next chapter.

Serves 6–8

Ingredients:

100g brown sugar
60g softened butter
2–3 slices peeled pineapples,
cut 1cm thick and diced
(I think 1cm squared works best)
1 cup self-raising flour
¼ tsp bicarbonate of soda
1 tsp ground cardamom*
110g castor sugar
60g butter
2 tbsp golden syrup
2 large eggs
½ cup milk

Method:

Melt the brown sugar and butter stirring together over a low heat in a heavy based saucepan until totally blended together.

Pour the sugar mixture into a well-greased 20cm cake tin covering the whole base.

Scatter the diced pineapple neatly over the brown sugar mixture, right to the edges.

Sift together flour, bicarbonate of soda and cardamom in a bowl.

Mix in the castor sugar and make a well in the centre of the bowl.

Melt together the butter and golden syrup and pour this into the well of dry ingredients with the eggs and milk.

Beat all ingredients together with a wooden spoon and pour into a cake tin over the diced pineapple and bake at 175°C for just under an hour or until a skewer inserted into the cake comes out clean.

If you think the cake risks being burnt on the outside during the cooking process, pop a bit of metal foil across it.

Once out of the oven, allow the cake to stand and cool for five minutes before inverting it onto a plate, ensuring all the sticky pineapple pieces fall into place or you may have to do a bit of rebuilding (I often do).

This goes beautifully with some whipped cream flavoured with a little essence of rose water, old-fashioned or yogurt.

*I grind cardamom pods in my coffee grinder for this, and tend to err on the generous side with the quantity.

Matcha 'green tea' ice cream

This ice cream is indeed green. (Avocado green in fact.) You might serve it, for novelty, with one of the above cakes.

Serves 4–6

Ingredients:
3 tbsp hot water
1 tbsp matcha
2 egg yolks
5 tbsp sugar
¾ cup milk
¾ cup heavy cream,
whipped

Method:

Mix water with *matcha* in a bowl and put to one side.

Whisk egg yolks lightly in a saucepan.

Add sugar and mix well.

Gradually add milk and mix well.

Put the pan over a low heat, stirring constantly while the mixture thickens and then remove from the heat.

Half fill your sink with cold water and stand the pan in to cool the mixture.

Add the green tea mixture to the egg and sugar mixture in the pan and mix well while it is still cooling in the iced water.

Gently fold in the whipped cream.

Pour the mixture into an ice cream maker and freeze per machine's instructions.

Alternatively pour into a container and freeze, stirring every hour or so.

Chapter 7

Tea cocktails and canapés

Here follows a range of ideas (alcoholic and not) that may amuse your palate. In some way or form they all are concoctions connected to tea by dint of their content or a bit of steeping or infusing. They are drinks to perk you up whatever the season and whatever your taste, and can be enjoyed at any time in the day.

Iced vanilla tea
Serves 4

Ingredients:
1 vanilla bean
1 tbsp tea leaves of your choice
Orange pekoe would be mine.
1 tbsp castor sugar
boiling water
quantity ice cubes
2 drops rose water or orange
blossom water (optional)

Method:
Slit open vanilla bean lengthways with a sharp knife and place in a teapot with the tea leaves and sugar.

Add boiling water and steep for a few moments.

Allow tea to cool and then add rose or orange water and pour over ice in tall glasses.

Sweet matcha lemonade
Serves: 4–6

Ingredients:
½ lemon
2 heaped tsp sweet matcha (If you can only find standard matcha use that and add sugar to taste)
2 cups water
sliced lemon for garnish
quantity ice

Method:
Combine juice from the ½ lemon, the *matcha* tea and 2 cups of water.

Mix thoroughly and pour over ice.

Garnish with sliced lemon.

Cardamom cooler
This takes its inspiration from Rajasthan. It is a wonderful party drink. And it is multi-purpose working brilliantly served both hot or cold. Serves 1

Ingredients:

120ml unsweetened tinned pineapple juice
4 cardamom pods (or 1 tsp cardamom powder)
15ml freshly squeezed lemon juice
4 tbsp crushed ice
2 tbsp brandy (or rum)
additional cardamom pods and mint leaves for decoration

Method:

Place all the ingredients in a blender and whiz until combined, and then pour into a cocktail glass.

As mentioned above, this drink actually works just as well hot, and cinnamon may be added. Put all the ingredients except the brandy (and ice!) into a saucepan and gently warm for 20 minutes or so, then add brandy.

Green tea latte (cold)

Green tea lattes are novel and this recipe is just about popping the ingredients into a blender and pressing the button (and adding some rum if you wish).

Serves 2

Ingredients:

1 tsp matcha (powdered green tea)
1 tbsp warm water
1 cup cold, unsweetened soya milk
1 cup ice
1 tbsp honey
optional: light rum (to taste)

Method:

Make up a paste with the *matcha* powder and warm water.

Put soya milk, ice, honey and *matcha* mix into blender and blend for about a minute.

Scrape every last drop into your favourite latte glass, (or tea cup) and enjoy.

Lemon mint vodka

Serves: Here you are preparing a whole bottle, so it is up to you how many guests it will serve.

(I am counting on your indulgence here, as lemon mint vodka is not quite 'tea'. However as some steeping is involved while the mint leaves suffuse the vodka, an interesting infusion is created.)

Ingredients:
750ml bottle of vodka
rind from 1 lemon
10 mint leaves

Method:
Drop lemon rind and washed and dried mint leaves into the bottle of vodka and refrigerate for one week.

(Taste test after two or three days.)

Pour into a glass and drink neat or with a mixer.

(A good idea is to store the bottle in the freezer, which gives the vodka a wonderful rich velvety texture.)

Lemon mint gin
Gin works just as well as vodka in the above preparation.

Raspberry vodka
My sister Melanie runs this up.
Makes approximately one bottle.

Ingredients:
3–4 cups raspberries
1 tbsp sugar
750ml bottle of vodka
1 freezer
A couple of months up your sleeve for steeping

Melanie's method:
Fill a large storage jar (say 1–1.5L) with well-packed in raspberries.

Add 1 tbsp sugar and fill up with vodka.

Leave for a couple of months occasionally turning jar upside down.

Strain vodka (it should be very dark red).

Put about 4 inches of the nectar (a bit like the *zavarka* essence in Russian tea brewing) into a new bottle, and dilute with vodka (by now it should be a lovely pale pink colour).

Keep in freezer and drink neat.

Bloody Mary with Kaffir lime leaves and lemongrass

The Kaffir lime leaves and lemongrass prompted me to include this delicious recipe. It is a twist on a Bloody Mary and a great energy booster either at the end of the day or at the beginning: especially after the big night you shouldn't have had!

Serves 1

Ingredients:

60ml gin
6 Kaffir lime leaves, finely torn up leaves of 1 small sprig rosemary, finely chopped
½ stick of lemongrass, finely chopped
squeeze of lemon juice
couple of dashes of Worcestershire sauce
tabasco to taste
rock salt and cracked pepper
top with V8 or tomato juice

Method:

Put all the ingredients into a glass (over ice if desired), stir and serve.

Canapés

Portuguese cheese balls, Pão de queijo

Courtesy of my friend, Irene. These are delightful cheese balls-cum-puffs. They are light and crunchy with warm soft centres, and as they are made with arrowroot they are great for those who are wheat intolerant. You can make up a quantity of the balls and freeze them and call on them when needed.

Makes 10–20

Ingredients:

½ cup milk
1 tbsp butter
230g arrowroot
1 tsp salt
1 egg
150g grated cheddar cheese

100g grated parmesan cheese
extra cold milk (for use when
kneading dough)

Method:

Heat oven to 220°C.

Warm milk and melt butter.

Place mixture into a large mixing bowl.

Mix in arrowroot and salt and then allow to sit and cool. The mixture can be quite lumpy resembling breadcrumbs.

Once cool, add egg, then cheese and knead to a dough (At this point you may require a little bit of cold milk to assist with the consistency.)

Roll dough into small balls and place them on a greased tray and put into the pre-heated oven for 10 or so minutes (until you see them turning golden brown).

Drop the oven temperature to about 120°C and leave in the oven for a further five or so minutes.

Remove from oven and cool them for a few moments.

Pop them on a platter and serve.

Keep an eye on them. You will discern how long you like them to be cooked for. In our family there is a big appetite for super-crunchy well-cooked cheese. You may prefer your cheese a little softer. And there is plenty of scope to use different cheeses and any spice, such as paprika, to add extra flavour.

Mutabbal, or moutabel a hot Palestinian dip

(This is a spicier version of *baba gannouj*.)
Serves 4

Ingredients:
2 large eggplants,
or 3 medium eggplants
2–3 cloves garlic, minced
2–3 tbsp tahini*
juice 1 lemon
1–3 chopped green chillies
½ tsp sea salt
pinch of pepper
1 tbsp olive oil

Method:

Remove the rough top of the plants.

With a sharp knife score them right around their middles length-wise.

Roast for 30 minutes at 200°C.

Remove from the oven and when cool enough peel, or scoop out all the flesh.

Chop up flesh coarsely and set aside.

In a food processor combine tahini*, garlic and chilli.

Add eggplant flesh and blend well.

Add in olive oil and blend further.

Remove from processor and place in serving bowl. Stir in lemon juice and sprinkle over salt and pepper to taste.

Serve with warm pita (or biscuits of your choice).

*Tahini is very simple to make. See following recipe:

Tahini
Makes 1½ cups

Ingredients:
5 cups sesame seeds
1½ cups olive or vegetable oil

Method:

Toast sesame seeds in a 180°C oven for 5–10 minutes tossing regularly to guard against burning.

Add to olive or vegetable oil in a blender and blend for a couple of minutes. That's it.

Caraway and onion biscuits
These are a little fiddly but worth the effort.
Serves 8–10

Ingredients:
1½ cups flour (preferably wholemeal) flour
1 tsp baking powder

¾ tsp salt
50g chilled and finely diced butter
1 large brown onion very finely
chopped
½ cup (approximately) skim milk
2–3 tsp caraway seeds

Method:

Heat oven to 230°C.

In a bowl lightly mix together the flour, baking powder, salt and butter until they resemble fine breadcrumbs.

Lightly mix in half the chopped onion and the milk.

Put dough onto a lightly floured surface and pat into a square (approximately 18cm).

Cut into nine equal squares.

Sprinkle with remaining onion and caraway seeds.

Transfer to baking sheet and bake for 20 minutes.

Best served straight away.

Chapter 8

Beguiling brews and infusions

Dried flowers, roots and bark have been brewed into consumable hot liquid for centuries to enhance health and provide remedies for sickness and disorder. Today there are literally hundreds of infusions and brews. I encountered 'horsetail' tea, for example, something of a surprise although I did not buy it. And when, on spec, I brewed some rosemary from our garden a significant reward was in the making.

Steeped rosemary

Steeped rosemary is absolutely delicious hot or cold and is bursting with healthy properties. When I have had a cup or two, I pour what remains from the pot into a highball glass and I sip on it at room temperature during the remainder of the day. It's much more interesting than tap water and contributes to that required daily intake of fluid.

I have since learned that rosemary is like a wonder herb. It is said to fight against rheumatism, arthritis, diabetes, chronic pain and long-term stress. It is also anti-inflammatory and it assists circulation. And that's not all. It has easily digestible calcium in it and it works against hair loss, depression, anxiety and the inability to thrive. It also is said to improve memory, concentration, outlook and energy. Little surprise I enjoy it so much. What's not to like?

Steeped rosemary
Makes 1 pot

Ingredients:
3 small sprigs rosemary (3x10cm)
boiling water
honey (if you need a sweetener)

Method:
Rinse rosemary briefly under running water; pop it into your favourite teapot and steep for five minutes.

Norway

When I asked my Norwegian friend, Tone, about any specific Norwegian tea practices she told me that little tea drinking is done in her country but that 'birch tea' does feature.

83

Birch tea
Makes 1 pot

Ingredients:
6–8 small twigs from the tips
of branches of birch
2 cups of water

Method:
Take twigs, crush them in a mortar and pestle, and immerse them in simmering water for 2–4 minutes.

The water will turn amber, is full of nutrients and ready then to be enjoyed.

Alternatively birch tea may be made up using small scrapings of birch bark prepared as with the branch tips. (Birch powder and flakes are available in health food shops for more ready access.)

Please be warned that this is not a drink for anyone who has any problems relating to aspirin, as birch has similar chemical compounds.

Birch and the promotion of hair growth
I have also read that a paste made from birch bark when applied to the scalp, can promote hair growth.

Steeped lemongrass and ginger
Among my friends and relations in Sydney this tea is a confirmed favourite. It takes a moment to prepare and is fabulously refreshing either hot or cold.
Makes 1 pot

Ingredients:
diced lemon grass (the last
3cm of a single stick)
diced ginger
(3–6cm cubed, unpeeled)
boiling water

Method:
Steep lemongrass and ginger in a pot of boiling water for 3–5 minutes. It's then ready to go.

Kombucha tea

A craze concerning this variety of tea arose in Sydney in the 80s and 90s and I for one fell victim to its beguiling promises: eternal life (naturally), strong hair, a flawless complexion, strong heart, and so on. We all went mad for it: had brews of it in the back of our refrigerators, and the breakfast table would have it sitting there as proud as it was ugly every morning.

I have learned now that there is limited scientific information supporting any suggested health benefits of *Kombucha* although there are several centuries of anecdotal accounts supporting the notion of its health benefits. *Kombucha* is available commercially but we all made it at home by fermenting tea using a visible, solid mass of yeast and bacteria that formed the *Kombucha* 'culture' which was and is referred to as the 'mushroom' or the 'mother'. It looked a little like a giant dead abalone.

Morocco

Moroccans use highly ornate teapots (often in engraved silver) and crystal glasses in the preparation and serving of tea, although traditionally Moroccans prepared tea in a samovar like the Russians. Usually a gunpowder tea is used. After brewing, the tea is heavily sweetened with sugar and flavoured with a touch of mint. The teapot is held high in the air while pouring the tea into the small, delicate glasses. This impressive feat is made possible by the long and slender curved spout on the Moroccan teapot (and no doubt a lot of practice). Apparently this custom developed when practitioners serving the tea attempted to cool it as it was poured from ever increasing heights, making it palatable more swiftly. Mint tea is an excellent complement to rich and spicy Moroccan cooking.

Moroccan mint tea
Serves 1

Ingredients:
1 tsp gunpowder green tea
1 sprig mint leaves
2–3 cups water
1 tsp sugar or honey to taste

Method:
Steep tea and mint in a pot
for 3–5 minutes.
Add honey or sugar as required.

South America

Yerba maté
'Liquid vegetable of the gaucho' or, 'Drink of the gods'.

I could not resist including this brew I found during my fact-finding. It dates back to the sixteenth century. To my astonishment I found it in a health food shop in downtown Sydney recently. Its flavour is very mild, rather similar to green tea even though it is not a tea as such, rather an infusion.

Yerba maté is itself a small tree native to the subtropical highlands of Brazil, Paraguay, Uruguay and Argentina. Throughout much of South America, its leaves are infused in water in a dried calabash *calabaza* gourd (like a pumpkin) and sipped through a filtered straw, called a *bombilla*.

This healthy brew is considered 'the drink of the gods' by many indigenous South Americans, and is a staple in the diets of many South American cattlemen, or 'gauchos'. It is a food product of high nutritional value that can withstand the rigours of life on the range. More particularly it has a very high caffeine content, so keeps its drinkers mentally alert. So prevalent is the consumption of *yerba maté* in South America, that maté bars are as widespread as coffee shops in the USA, teahouses in England, and *chaiwallah* stands in India. Traditionally, *maté* is shared among family and close friends. The gourd and *bombilla* are passed around and around and refilled from time to time, while a spirit of camaraderie is enjoyed.

Tibet

Butter tea

Meanwhile in Tibet you may drink tea brewed with yak's milk, butter and salt and, if you are fortunate enough, churned by a monk! This tea is known as butter tea, or *po cha*.

Drinking butter tea is a regular part of Tibetan life. Before work, a Tibetan will typically down several bowlfuls of it, and it is always what is served to guests. Nomads are said to often drink up to 40 cups of it a day. Since butter is the main ingredient, the tea is very warming, provides lots of energy, and is particularly suited to high altitudes. The butter also helps prevent chapped lips. Brilliant.

Tibetan protocol

According to Tibetan custom, butter tea is drunk haltingly in separate sips, and after each sip the host refills the bowl to the brim. Thus, a guest never drains his bowl fully: rather, it is constantly topped up. If a visitor does not wish to drink, the best thing to do is leave the tea untouched until the time comes to take ones leave, and then one swiftly drains the bowl. In this way etiquette is observed and the host will not be offended.

Chapter 9

Tea history

Tea has played a significant role in the history and traditions of many cultures. From ancient China and Japan to the Indian sub-continent, the width of the British Empire at its height and the expanses of Africa, tea has brought people together in the shared pleasure of a good brew.

China

The 'way of tea'

The Chinese tea ceremony, also called the Chinese 'way of tea' is an entrenched cultural activity involving the ceremonial preparation and presentation of tea. The so-called 'way of tea' has been influenced across millennia by Taoism, Buddhism and Confucianism.

In China today, tea is frequently brewed using the meditative *Gong Fu* method. This very formal, ritualised approach to tea preparation dates back to the *Míng* Dynasty (1368–1644 AD). The term *Gong Fu* refers to skill gained through practice: that is expertise derived not from learning but from experience. While the term *Gong Fu* might signify the serious practice of any art form, such as the martial art of *Kung Fu*, *Gong Fu Cha* refers to the elaborate preparation of tea using miniature *Yixing* pots (about 100–150ml) and petite cups. (The same cups that delighted Europeans in the seventeenth century.)

Yixing tea ware is named after the purple clay it is made from, which comes from *Yixing* in China's *Jiangsu* province. Everything in a *Gong Fu* tea service is small and delicate, placing emphasis on the elegance of the tea. Oolongs (tea whose leaves are partially oxidised prior to drying) or *pu-erh* tea are the preferred tea in the *Gong Fu* ritual; they are steeped repeatedly to intensify the developing flavour as the leaves gradually unfurl.

Tea-drinking customs

Tea preparation and consumption has many purposes: among these as a demonstration of respect, at family gatherings for example or to express apology or gratitude. In a traditional Chinese wedding ceremony, typically both the bride and groom kneel in front of their parents and serve them tea in thanks for all that has been done for them during their lives. The parents will drink a small amount of tea, and then ceremoniously give the bride and groom a red envelope, which symbolises a wish for good fortune.

At a family wedding sharing tea also inevitably connects families. In the past the patriarch may have had more than one wife and so understandably there was no guarantee that all family members would necessarily have been on good terms. The sharing of tea provided a much sought after opportunity to show acceptance and tolerance.

Background and some amateur etymology

Tea has been drunk in China for thousands and thousands of years. It is the birthplace of tea. It was first found in the southwestern region that has both a tropical and sub-tropical climate. Huge, 2,700 year old wild tea trees and 800 year-old cultivated trees can still be found there.

Up until the eighth century BC tea, (*Camellia sinensis*) was known as *tú*. The word *tú* is not a Chinese word as such. It is a 'pinyin' word. Pinyin is the formal system for transliterating Chinese into the Latin alphabet and

was introduced in 1958. It makes Chinese much more accessible to Westerners, and presumably it has led to the term 'pidgin'. Pidgin English is a perversion of English that has evolved as non-English speakers have gradually pieced together the [new] language as they learn it, overlaying it with their own accent.

Char

There is need to query the link between our everyday word 'tea' and *tú*, or the Hindi word 'chai' and the other contemporary Chinese word in pinyin for tea, *chá*. In England you still hear the slang, 'Come and have a cup o' char!' At least it was still extensively used in the 70s and 80s when I was living there and certainly in the 40s and 50s as my father attests.

My father went into the army at 17 and was a captain by the time he was 20 and spent much time between 1944 and 1948 in Egypt, Palestine and Germany.

He reminded me of the following:
'Napoleon famously said that an army marches on its stomach. The British army also marched on brew-ups or char. Every tank, armoured car, scout car or truck had its own 'billican' [sic] for instant use when halted. Char was always on the menu in Egypt, Palestine or Germany. It was a matter of skill to produce a brew when halted, even if only for a few minutes.'

And, according to my father, while brewing or sipping their char, the troops may have been humming the much-loved homespun ditty:

*'I like a nice cup of tea with my dinner
And a nice cup of tea with my tea
And at half past eleven
My idea of heaven
Is a nice cup of tea.'*

Míng
The Chinese word, *míng*, (also pinyin) referring to porcelain is in colloquial use; however, it was actually used to indicate tea itself when it was popularised throughout Ancient China.

Today *míng* is still used to denote tea in Taiwan and the People's Republic of China.

Without too much elaboration, the word for tea followed the evolutionary steps (in pinyin) of *chá, jiǎ, shè, míng* and finally *chuǎn*.

Tea names
Take a look at the following country names and associated tea names that show how many of them are still holding fast to derivatives from *tê* and *chá*. I find it really interesting how these simple core words have spread so far and are still in usage.

Derivatives from tê

Africkaans:	tee
Armenian:	tey
Catalan:	te
Czech:	té
Danish:	te
Dutch:	thee
Esperanto:	teo
Estonian:	tee
Finnish:	tee
French:	thé
German:	Tee
Hebrew:	te
Hungarian:	tea
Icelandic:	te
Indonesian:	teh
Italian:	tè
Khmer:	tae
Korean:	ta
Latvian:	tēja
Malay:	teh
Norwegian:	te
Occitan:	tè
Sesotho:	tea/cha
Sinhalese:	té
Spanish:	té
Swedish:	te
Welsh:	te

Derivatives from chá

Albanian:	çaj
Amharic:	shai
Arabic:	chāy
Azerbajani:	çay
Bosnian:	čaj
Croatian:	čaj
Czech:	čaj
English:	cha, chai, char
Persian:	chay
Georgian:	chai
Greek:	tsái
Hindi:	cāy
Japanese:	cha
Khasi:	sha
Korean:	cha
Kurdish:	ça
Malayalam:	chaaya
Mongolian:	tsai
Portuguese:	chá
Romanian:	ceai
Russian:	chai
Serbian:	ĉaj
Slovak:	ĉaj
Thai:	cha
Tibetan:	ja
Turkish:	çay
Uzbek:	choy

Additional notes:
The different articulations of the word for tea fall into two distinct groups and reveal from which particular Chinese culture all the non-Chinese nations (us) absorbed their tea and tea culture.

The first is *te*-derived (Min Chinese dialects) and the other, as seen, is *chá* -derived (Mandarin, Cantonese and other non-Min Chinese dialects).

India and the Arab world would likely have inherited their tea cultures from the Cantonese or southwestern Mandarin speakers.

Northern Mandarin speakers carried tea culture to Russia.

The Portuguese, who were the first Europeans to import tea took the Cantonese *chá*, as used in their trading posts in the south of China, especially Macau.

The first tea to reach Britain was traded by the Dutch from the Fujian province that uses *te*, and while later on tea went through Canton which uses *chá*, the Fujianese pronunciation continued to be the more popular

Customs and legends surrounding the Chinese tea ceremony

Napkin folding

At any tea ceremony the folding of the napkins was highly significant and done in order to ward off bad Qi.

(My mother must have realised this, as she is a fastidious napkin-folder.)

Finger tapping

There is a delightful ancient custom for thanking the person who has offered you your tea. Once your cup has been filled, you may choose to knock on the table to express your gratitude. (It is common to do so in southern China, but in other regions it is a custom only really followed when you are not in a position to say thank you: maybe because you are chatting....) Your middle three fingers would be used for the purpose.

The legend behind this relates back to the *Qing* Dynasty when Emperor *Qian Long* travelled his empire in disguise (as was his practice) to keep an eye on his subjects. His entourage was never allowed to disclose his identity. One day however in public, the Emperor, still in disguise, filled his servant's teacup after serving himself. This bestowed a great honour on the servant whose spontaneous response would normally have been to kneel in gratitude. However, as he could not risk exposing the identity of his esteemed Emperor, he simply bent his fingers on the table as a sign of respect to him. (The middle finger represents the head of the servant and the index and fourth fingers, his arms.)

GoA, the God of Agriculture

The God of Agriculture just one of the legendary discoverers of tea, GoA, was worshipped in prehistoric China for inventing agriculture and medicine, and he was also said to be the discoverer of tea. (There are many other legends to be found relating to who may have discovered tea, so this claim is not by any means definitive.) However in GoA's *Book of Herbs* it says that GoA personally tasted hundreds of herbs and that in a single day, he was poisoned no fewer than 72 times. Fortunately he discovered the tea tree and used its leaves to neutralise the poison. How fortunate for him and for his followers who went on to benefit from the magical qualities of tea he had discovered.

Modern culture

In modern China virtually every household (down to the simplest mud hut) has a set of tea implements for brewing tea. These implements are symbols of welcome for visitors or neighbours. Traditionally, and today, a visitor is expected to sit while he or she sips his or her tea. It is construed as rude to stand.

There are countless types of tea routinely kept in the pantry; green tea, oolong tea (also known as blue tea), red tea, white tea, yellow tea, *pu-erh* tea and probably herbals too such as chrysanthemum.

There is an interesting distinction to be made here. While Westerners define tea by the colour of the leaf used in tea making, the Chinese refer to the colour of the liquor (the brew) in their definition. Thus what I as a Westerner would call black tea, a Chinese person would call red.

Japan
Japan's tea story is inextricably bound to that of China however it has developed its own identity.

Sencha
The first documented evidence of tea in Japan dates from the ninth century when the Buddhist monk, *Eichū*, imported it from China. *Eichū* personally prepared *sencha* for the then Emperor Saga in 815, who must have enjoyed it greatly as within the year (by imperial decree) tea plantations were being developed all over the Empire.

Sencha was a cake of compressed green tea that was steamed and formed into bricks for storage and trade. The drink was prepared as required by roasting the cake or brick, pulverising it in a mortar, and then brewing it together with other herbs and flavourings.

Tencha and matcha
By the twelfth century the style of preparing tea known as *tencha* was recorded, again introduced into Japan from China by a Buddhist monk, this one named *Eisai*. (History relates that *Eisai's* tea seeds went on to produce highly desirable tea.) The fine powdered tea used in this preparation was called *matcha*. It was placed in a bowl and hot water was poured over it, and the two were whipped together into a 'froth of jade'.

Maintaining health by drinking tea
Eisai wrote a book *Maintaining Health by Drinking Tea* in 1211. He wrote:

'Tea is a miraculous medicine for the maintenance of health. Tea has an extraordinary power to prolong life. Anywhere a person cultivates tea, long life will follow. In ancient and modern times, tea is the elixir that creates the mountain-dwelling immortal.'

Matcha

Matcha as noted already is much in use and is readily available today. Apparently it has more antioxidants 'pound-for-pound' than blueberries, gojiberries, pomegranates, orange juice or spinach. It is also meant to boost metabolism and help reduce cholesterol levels. As a green tea it also helps blood pressure and blood sugar; it kills bacteria, fights halitosis, and carcinogenic bacteria. It strengthens blood vessel walls and has fluoride in it so aids the battle against cavities and the vitamin E in it regulates aging. It is the most remarkable of tonics, as determined by the Chinese long long ago. But do beware, *matcha* is very high in caffeine content (like *yerba maté*) so best not taken at night, if you are sensitive to caffeine, unless you intend on being awake into the wee small hours.

Up until the twelfth century in Japan tea drinking had mainly been mainly focused on curative remedies and religious rituals, but I have read that by the thirteenth century during the reign of the Kamakura Shogunate and the samurai warrior class tea, and all its attendant luxuries, took on a life of its own. To have high quality tea was considered a mark of distinction among the warrior class, and passion to posses it was rife. Then came tea-tasting parties rather in the fashion that we might today have a wine-tasting party with a competitive edge. The rewards were lavish if you could identify the tea of the best quality. (It turns out that the tea grown from *Eisai's* seeds imported centuries before was deemed to be far and away the best.)

The Japanese tea ceremony

Murata Jukō

Many different schools of the Japanese 'tea ceremony' have evolved over time. *Murata Jukō*, a student of Zen, is known in *cha-no-yu* (tea ceremony) history as the foremost developer of the early 'tea ceremony' as a spiritual practice, and is therefore generally considered to be the founder of the Japanese 'way of tea'. He set out the principles of harmony, respect, purity and tranquility; all still central to today's Japanese 'tea ceremony'. *Cha-no-yu* (or *chadō* or *sado*) is a traditional ritual, often performed in a bamboo teahouse, in which *matcha* is ceremonially prepared by a skilled practitioner and served to a small group of guests in a peaceful setting. *Cha-no-yu* (literally hot water for tea) usually refers to a single ceremony or ritual, while *sado* or *chadō* ('the way of tea') refer more precisely to the study or doctrine of the tea ceremony.

Wabi-sabi

Wabi-sabi is the name given to the particular aesthetic surrounding the tea ceremony.

Wabi represents the inner or spiritual experience of life, emphasising quiet and sober reflection, characterised by humility and restraint: this based within a simple, unadorned environment, the *sabi*, in order to celebrate the enduring 'mellow beauty that time and care impart to material objects'.

It was believed that coming to terms with 'emptiness' was a vital step towards spiritual awakening, and espousing imperfection was seen as a healthy way to accept our lesser 'ordinary' selves in the here and now. This would ultimately lead the humble and modest towards *satori* or enlightenment.

Ichi-go ichi-e, Sen no Rikyû and Takeno Jōō

By the sixteenth century tea drinking had spread to all levels of society in Japan. *Sen no Rikyû*, apparently the most widely known and revered figure in the history of the tea ceremony, followed his master, *Takeno Jōō's* concept of *ichi-go ichi-e*; a philosophy that each individual encounter should be prized, as it would only ever occur the once. He perfected the development of *chadō*, the 'way of tea', still practised today.

While the Japanese tea ceremony was heavily influenced by Chinese practices and Zen Buddhism, the extraordinarily precise formula for the tea ceremony known now evolved years later, quite distinct from the established Chinese practice of taking tea. In Japanese culture, every element of the tea ceremony, from the greeting of guests to the arrangement of flowers, even the architecture of the setting, is rigidly prescribed, requiring the host to be knowledgeable in a broad range of arts and disciplines. It is essential that the participants of the tea ceremony also be familiar with the proper gestures, phrases and actions required of them throughout the ceremony.

India

Tea drinking in India can be dated back as far as 750BC. It is now one of the largest tea producers in the world. It is easy to believe, with a population today of 1.22 billion, that it is one of the largest consumers of tea in the world, and the fourth largest exporter (after Sri Lanka, Kenya and China). Today the tea names of Assam, Darjeeling and Ceylon are part of our tea lexicon.

Assam

The state of Assam is the world's largest tea-growing region, lying on either side of the Brahmaputra River, and bordering Bangladesh and Burma (Myanmar). Along with southern China, Assam is the only other region in the world with native tea plants. Its climate is tropical. During the monsoon period it may rain as much as 300mm (12 inches) a day and temperatures can peak at 40°C (103°F). Perfect for the leaf.

Assam is where the British East India Company began its cultivation of tea in the early 1800s. Its first recorded shipment of tea was sent from there to England in 1838, one year after Queen Victoria ascended to the throne. As previously noted Assam teas are frequently used in breakfast teas and blends and Queen Victoria was besotted with breakfast tea and was very much a force behind its popularity. Although Assam is usually connoted by black teas, it does produce smaller quantities of green and white teas.

Darjeeling

The tea-growing region of Darjeeling is much smaller and grows much less tea than Assam per acre. It is colder and higher so growth is slower. However it is India's best-known tea and for multitudes their best loved as well.

Kanchenjunga, one of the world's tallest peaks, rises just to the east of Darjeeling. Tea is cultivated there on slopes of up to a staggering 60 or 70 degrees. This steepness provides natural drainage for the generous rainfall delivered by monsoon winds. Here tea is planted from approximately 550 metres (1,800 feet) to 1,900 metres (6,300 feet). This is staggeringly (no pun intended) almost two kilometres (or a mile). Tea can barely grow above 1,800 metres (6,000 feet). The higher it is grown, the thinner the tea's body and more concentrated its flavour. Other determining factors (as for all teas) are wind, sun, cloud, exposure, temperature, rain and soil chemistry.

Darjeeling's individuality

Most of the tea plants used in Darjeeling are of the China or China-hybrid type and rarely if ever found outside China and Japan except in Darjeeling and the Caucasus. They are more resistant to the cold than other Indian teas, their leaves are smaller and their yield considerably lower.

The young shoots are harvested as soon as they are ready which means hand-plucking each bush every four to eight days throughout the growing season. A typical plant produces only about 100 grams per year (four ounces) of made tea. This is less than a third of the yield generated by Assam plants grown on the plains. Furthermore each kilogram of Darjeeling consists of over 20,000 individual shoots. This figure is almost too large for me to grasp as is all the related data about leaf picking. Each different batch of fresh leaves brought into a factory requires highly tuned processing into intricate varieties to maximise its full potential. A mountainous job if you will forgive another pun. The depth and magic of the tales surrounding Darjeeling tea seem infinite. The subject is worthy of an entire book. Suffice it to say that First Flush Darjeeling is the world's most expensive tea.

Ceylon tea (Sri Lankan)

Ceylon Tea was developed and became widely known in the west in the nineteenth century thanks due largely to a Scot named James Taylor. He moved to Ceylon in the mid-1800s having heard about the lush island and there he undertook the cultivation of tea but only as a secondary business to that of coffee growing. Woefully his coffee plantation was to be wiped out by a leaf disease, 'coffee-rust-fungus', one to which the modest tea leaf was immune, thus paving its way to becoming the premier commodity in Ceylon.

Ceylon's teas gardens are on slopes ranging from 450 metres (1,500 feet) to 2,500 metres (8,000 feet). And, akin to Darjeeling, the leaves produced vary considerably. Low-grown teas have good colour and strength and are often used in blending. Mid-grown leaves give stronger colour and flavour, while high-grown teas give a golden liquor and intense flavour, which is how Ceylon black teas are generally characterised. That is by an intense colour and crisp aroma.

(Some tea estates in Ceylon/Sri Lanka also produce silver tip white tea.)

Indian tea also on occasion a vegetable

In the sixteenth century a Dutch explorer, *Jan Huyghen van Linschoten*, noted that the Indians were using tea as a vegetable side dish and cooking it up with garlic and oil and then stewing the leaves to make a drink. This bears a passing resemblance to a Chinese mixture dating back to the *T'ang* Dynasty when tea leaves were brewed for variety with plums and onions.

Cartage

In the seventeenth century, the journey between India and Britain took between 12 and 15 months. Transport costs and prohibitive taxes meant that early on tea was a drink only the significantly wealthy could enjoy as already noted. Late in the eighteenth century taxes were reduced and it became a drink for Everyman. Also, when the Suez Canal was opened in 1869, this journey was reduced to a mere three months.

The British East India Company, tea and opium

John Barrow wrote in the Quarterly Magazine of 1836:

'....it is a curious circumstance that we grow poppy in our Indian territories to poison the people of China in return for a wholesome beverage which they prepare almost exclusively for us.'

In the late eighteenth and early nineteenth century the British East India Company (established in 1600) set about trading Bengal opium for Chinese tea. (The Mogul Emperor had granted the company trading rights in the early seventeenth century.) While Chinese tea was highly prized, Britain had little to offer in exchange, thus its decline into trading it with opium. The two crops' interdependence carried vast financial and political weight.

For one thing the British East India Company forced Indian farmers to destroy their other crops in order to cultivate opium. Then it literally crushed the Indian cotton industry to supplant it with English cotton and yet more opium cultivation. And this is only a fraction of the whole catastrophic picture. Through crop control, managed by the East India Company, England gained both financial and political supremacy in India and the ignominy of being the first country to promote drug addiction by deploying military force. The legacy: a shameful one of poverty and addiction amidst much else.

In England meanwhile, banks were being established on the back of opium and tea trading. Fortunes were being made and upheld by it, as were grand houses and the opulent life-styles being conducted therein.

Simultaneously the exchanges between China and Britain developed into fully-fledged conflict described neatly as the 'Opium Wars' in our history books.

These wars significantly altered these countries' existing trade relationship. Whereas in 1839 all the tea drunk in Britain was ostensibly Chinese, by the 1860s 85 percent of it came from India and Ceylon and only 12 percent from China.

Africa

Rooibos

Rooibos is Afrikaans for red bush. The red bush produces leaves that make up what is known variously as rooibos tea, bush tea, redbush tea, South African red tea or simply red tea. It has long slender leaves rather like pine needles. In South Africa rooibos has been popular for generations but it is now drunk across the globe. It is sometimes spelled rooibosch in accordance with Dutch etymology, but pronounced the same as *rooibos*; that is roy-bos. I learned about it when first pregnant many years ago. It is meant, beyond countless other healthy properties, to be excellent for pregnancy and breastfeeding.

Honeybush tea

Honeybush tea is indigenous to South Africa. It is herbal and has many health-giving properties. It is also known as Heuningtee, Bergtee, Boertee, Bossiestee and Bushtea.

Kenya

The British introduced tea to Kenya, Tanzania and Uganda unlike other of their dominions such as India, Hong Kong and Pakistan that had pre-existing tea cultures. Production of tea in Kenya was first undertaken in the early twentieth century and seedlings from India were used. Now Kenya is one of the world's major producers. (Approximately 240 million kilograms [240,000 tonnes] a year.)

Kenya is able to produce tea all year round because of its location close to the equator. The tea is picked every 17 days and is grown between 1,500 and 2,200 metres (5,000 and 7,000 feet). Most tea estates are situated near the equator although some older ones are in the Great Rift Valley in western Kenya.

CTC and 'Pecco'

Kenyan tea is mostly black and used primarily in blending and tea bag production. Most of it is processed by the CTC (cut, tear and curl) method and comes in three main grades: Broken pekoe (also sometimes spelled 'pecco'), pekoe fannings, and pekoe dusts. The loose-leaf tea has a very strong flavour and is reddish in colour.

Tea grading

Western society uses what is called the orange pekoe grading system to classify black teas. The system is based upon the size of the processed and dried black leaves. It goes without saying that high-grade teas are produced using only the very best leaves, those obtained from new flushes. The size and wholeness of the leaves has a great bearing on the taste, clarity and the brewing time of the tea. This grading system is used for teas from Sri Lanka (Ceylon), India, Kenya (as above) and other tea-producing countries though not China.

Grades

I am much endeared to the following list of grades:

Whole leaf:

• SFTGOP: Super Fine Tippy Golden Flowery Orange Pekoe

• FTGFOP: Fine Tippy Golden Flowery Orange Pekoe

• TGFOP: Tippy Golden Flowery Orange Pekoe

Broken leaf (consisting of small leaves or pieces of large leaves):

• FTGBOP: Fine Tippy Golden Broken Orange Pekoe

• TGBOP: Tippy Golden Broken Orange Pekoe

• FBOP: Flowery Broken Orange Pekoe

• BOP: Broken Orange Pekoe

Fannings (consisting of even smaller sizes than the brokens):

• GFOF: Golden Flowery Orange Fannings

• GOF Golden Orange Fannings

Dust, the lowest grade, (consisting of small pieces of tea leaves and dust)

• D

It is easy to deduce, the more initials, the better the tea!

Chapter 10

Further tea miscellanea

Tea lifts us up when we need a boost, it fortifies, unites and sustains. Tea is all the colours of the rainbow and its myriad of practical applications have yet to be fully explored.

A background in colour

Camellia sinensis

Amazingly as already stated all standard tea as we know it comes from the one evergreen tea tree, *Camellia sinensis*, and depending on the process used, is manufactured into black, green, yellow, white or blue (oolong) tea. The quality of the leaves depends on when and where they are picked, the climate, the altitude and the composition of the soil.

Black tea

Black tea goes through the most processing. Once the leaves are picked they are spread out on trays to wither in the sun in temperatures of 25–30°C. The leaves are then gently rolled about which ruptures them and this releases their inner chemicals. These react with the air and the leaves begin to oxidise. At this point they are then put aside to rest. During oxidisation, the leaves darken and change from green to red and finally to black. After oxidising is complete, the leaves are dried and packaged. Assam, Darjeeling, Ceylon (Sri Lankan), Kenyan, orange pekoe and China blacks such as *Keemun* are all examples of black tea.

Blue (oolong) teas

Blue (oolong) teas are semi-oxidised leaves so follow the same process as for black tea but are withered or wilted more briefly. There are many varieties of oolong. The leaves may be shaken to cause a little bruising promoting light oxidisation after which they may be rolled either into tight knots or long, fine strands. The delicate oolong flavour derives from subtle handling and the location in which the leaves have been cultivated. Mount Wuyi, in the Fujian province of China, boasts the most expensive (oolong) tea available in that country. There you will find six-hundred-year old tea trees given the name Red Robe.

There are many other tea names like Red Robe which for me have a touch of magic such as *Tung-ting* (known too as *Dong Ding*) an oolong tea that comes from Taiwan.

In general, oolong leaves can range from being almost black to dark green according to how long they have been oxidised. Formosa is an example of oolong tea that has dark leaves and *Ti Kuan Yin* is an example of an oolong tea with green leaves.

Green tea

Green tea is considered by some to be the more natural tea as it is less processed. The oxidising process is entirely omitted. The younger leaves are harvested for green tea. They remain soft until they are steamed, roasted, rolled and left to dry. They may be rolled into different shapes: *sencha* tea is rolled into fine strands, while gunpowder leaves are rolled into pellets. Once the leaves are shaped, they are dried and packaged.

Sencha, gunpowder, *Po Lo Chun*, chrysanthemum and dragon well are examples of green tea.

Yellow tea

Yellow tea is produced when damp tea leaves are left to dry for longer than generally required for green tea. This leads them to turn yellow. This process lifts some of the grassy flavour (distasteful to some apparently) that often characterises green tea. Examples of yellow tea are *Junshan*, *Yinzhen*, *Huoshan* and *Meng Ding Huang ya*.

White tea

White tea, the youngest of the group, is so named because of the white hairs that cover the leaf buds that are used in its production. The leaves are picked before the buds have a chance to open, and they are spread out to wither in the fresh air and then they are dried. *Pai Mu Tan*, Silver Needle, Peony White and White Monkey Paw are examples of white teas.

Blending tea

Blending tea is much like blending wine, or so I have heard, as I have not practised this myself. A well-tuned palate is needed and extensive skill and knowledge. A practitioner needs years to acquire the requisite expertise for the task. When the blender-practitioners arrive at the tasting part of their duties, the same methods as wine tasting are employed. A mouthful of the tea, air breathed in, swirling and slurping and so on.

Tasseography

No book on tea could be complete without the inclusion of this word although I didn't know it until I looked it up. Also known as *tasseomancy* or *tassology*, it refers to 'the divination or fortune-telling method that interprets the patterns in tea leaves' (and also coffee grounds or wine sediments), or more simply, fortune telling. All three above terms derive from the French word *tasse* (cup) that comes from the similar Arabic word, *tassa*.

Guide to fortune telling or divining

After a cup of tea has been poured, without using a tea strainer, you drink or tip away the liquid. Your cup then needs to be shaken thoroughly and all remaining liquid drained off. You (the diviner) now look at the pattern of tea leaves in the cup and allow your imagination to play around with the shapes. The pattern might suggest a letter, a heart shape, or a ring possibly. With less obvious shapes you can make an intuitive interpretation, for example, a snake may suggest enmity or treachery, a spade effort and reward, a mountain a hurdle and so on.

The tea wizard

I have included here a short list of household hints concerning tea and its leaves, and it covers both the 'how-to' in regard to tea stains, and also how tea or its leaves might in fact assist you at home, further to all the other magnificent qualities it possesses that I have already touched on in this book.

Tea, the stain remover
– To remove a tea stain from white fabric, apply a few drops of lemon juice to it and then rinse away with cold water.

– To remove a tea stain from coloured fabric, (including silk or wool) apply egg yolk thinned down with warm water then rinse away as above.

– To remove tea stains from rugs or carpets, mix 50–50 methylated spirits and white wine (or white vinegar); soak the carpet or rug with the mixture and then dab dry with a clean cloth.

Tea, the enhancer
– To shine your mirrors or chrome simply use a cloth dipped in cold tea.

– Tired dark-coloured carpets? Brush with squeezed-dry infused leaves and then vacuum up.

– Tea is fabulous for your plants. Indoors or out of doors, scatter your leaves on them generously.

– Tea as a dyeing agent. Make up a strong brew and soak your fabric till it turns the colour you wish for.

Tea, the sous-chef
– Want to perk up the flavour of your dried fruits? Soak them in your favourite brew or similarly, poach fresh fruit in tea with honey or sugar and spices you like.

– Stuff fish with oolong or green tea before steaming.

– Marinate meat, tofu or seafood in cold tea for 30 minutes to enrich their flavour. This marinating method really works.

– Use *matcha* as a rub for grilled meats: apparently, besides enhancing the flavour, it will reduce the formation of carcinogens in charred or grilled meats especially where fatty cuts (such as those used in mince) are involved.

Conversion chart
1 cup (250ml)

Weights

25g	1oz
50g	2oz
75g	3oz
125g	4oz
250g	8oz
300g	10oz
400g	13oz
500g	1lb
1kg	2.2lb
1.5kg	3lb
2kg	4lb

Liquids

25ml	1fl oz
50ml	2fl oz
75ml	3fl oz
125ml	4fl oz
250ml	8fl oz
300ml	½ pint
400ml	14fl oz
500ml	17fl oz
1L	1¾ pints

Temperatures

110°C	225°F
180°C	350°F
220°C	425°F

Index

115

Acknowledgements

My greatest thanks to all my family and friends, particularly Ant, my husband, and Julie Gibbs and Ian Creber, whose tireless suppport was my oxygen during the development of *The Magic of Tea*.

My thanks also to Nicholas Shakespeare a brilliant author and biographer and much cherished friend who generously gave his time to reading *The Magic of Tea*, providing it with its wonderful foreword.

My thanks to May King Tsang, a certified tea specialist, who gave me her time, guidance and kindness, and who taught me an invaluable amount during my discovery of tea.

And most importantly, my gratitude to Jane Curry, my publisher, Sarah Plant, my editor, Cheryl Collins, the book's designer and production manager Karen Young, who have all brought their flare and professionalism to this enterprise and made it an exhilarating and rewarding experience. Thank you all so much.

2012